DOLLS

Other Main Street Pocket Guides

The Main Street Pocket Guide to
DOLLS

JEAN BACH

The Main Street Press

Pittstown, New Jersey

First Main Street edition, 1983

The Main Street Press
William Case House
Pittstown, New Jersey 08867

Printed in the United States of America

Library of Congress Cataloging in Publication Data

Bach, Jean.
    The Main Street pocket guide to dolls.

    (The Main Street pocket guide series)
    Bibliography: p. 252
    Includes index.
    1. Dolls—Collectors and collecting. I. Title.
NK4893.B28   1983   688.7′221   83-61593
ISBN 0-915590-36-0

Contents

How To Use This Book

The purpose of this book is to provide the collector with a visual identification guide to German, French, and American dolls and to supply descriptions of a wide variety of these dolls to facilitate the collector's often difficult task of identifying and authenticating new acquisitions. To this end, an attempt has been made to classify dolls (with the exception of paper dolls) according to **clearly visible and tactile characteristics.**

This guide, then, consists basically of dolls classified by material, type, and maker. The first part of the book offers a variety of dolls selected to demonstrate both the range of **materials** used in making dolls—from wood and cloth and wax to metal, bisque, and composition—and the many ways that such diverse materials are employed. With continued practice, even the beginning collector can learn to distingush, through touch and sight, these basic materials—except, perhaps, for rubber and gutta-percha which are remarkably alike.

The second part of the guide is categorized by **type.** Since doll makers throughout the years have consistently recreated the physical world in miniature—sometimes realistically, sometimes fancifully—the most visible characteristic of a doll is its approximation of a particular element of the real world. Our eyes (but not without the accumulated wisdom of experience) tell us what the doll is meant to simulate—be it a baby, a grown woman, a native of a foreign country, a well-known comic-strip character, or a famous movie actress.

Of the nineteen categories within this second section, a few have been classified by **function,** rather than by what the dolls are meant to simulate in the physical world. These include fashion dolls (section 16), mechanical dolls (section 20), and talking dolls (section 21), among others. These functions, like type and material, are clearly visible to even the untrained eye.

The third part of the book is classified according to many of the most **famous makers** in demand by collectors, ranging from such French and German firms as Jumeau and Kestner to such American manufacturers as Schoenhut, Fulper, and EFFanBEE. Implicit in this third section are the visual characteristics (in addition to the maker's marks) that the many dolls of a single manufacturer may share in common.

Use of this collector's guide is designed with ease, speed, and portability in mind. Suppose you spot an interesting cloth doll that appeals to you at a flea market or in an antiques shop. Perhaps the dealer has told you the obvious: "It is an old rag doll." But is it lithographed or handmade? Is it marked? Needle-molded? Stretched-over a mask? Can it be precisely dated? These are just a few of the questions you may want answers to.

By turning to the Color Key to Dolls (pp. 17-48), you will find among the color illustrations a photograph of a doll that bears a close resemblance to the one you are interested in—the visible characteristics, the basic form are similar. Under the color illustration will be found the number and name of its classification. By turning to the number and chapter heading in the body of the book which corresponds with the color photograph (i.e., 46. Martha J. Chase), you will be able to find either the identical doll or one very similar to it. By turning to the pages in the body of the book, you will discover, among other things, its maker, the date and place of manufacture, a concise and detailed description of the piece, and its approximate value. A careful inspection of the doll itself will also tell you a great deal, since often the maker's mark will be visible. (See the index to marks at the end of the book.)

Each of the 500 dolls discussed in this guide is treated in a separate numbered entry containing essential information. A typical entry is reproduced on p. 9, together with a list of all the basic elements contained in each entry of the book. Most of these elements are self-explanatory, but the reader should take note of several areas:

Eye Color: Eye color is assumed to be blue unless otherwise noted.

Clothing: The term "original clothing" does not imply that a doll was originally purchased wearing the clothing illustrated. Many, if not most, early dolls were dressed at home. The term is used to indicate that the antique clothing is original to the period of the doll and suitable for its type.

Articulation: The term "fully jointed" is used to indicate joints at shoulders, elbows, hips, knees, and wrists.

Marks: A double slant line (//) is used to indicate the beginning of a new line in a mark, since a single slant mark (/) sometimes occurs as part of a mark.

Terminology: Many of the entries may contain terms that are unfamiliar to beginning collectors. A glossary of terms is provided on p. 13.

Price Range: This is a treacherous area, so let no one fool you into thinking that any so-called price guide is a completely accurate means of determining a doll's value. Essentially, a doll is worth whatever a collector is willing to pay for it. Still, there have to be guidelines, and this guide offers not prices, per se, but **price ranges** based on the following considerations: (1) that the doll is in good condition; that is, with minor restoration as defined by recognized experts; (2) that the body and limbs are original to the head. The reader should also be aware that scarceness and demand, as well as size, are relevant to price. The price ranges suggested in this guide are coded as follows:

 A — $10,000 and over
 B — $3,000 to $10,000
 C — $1,000 to $3,000
 D — $500 to $1,000
 E — $100 to $500
 F — $100 or less

Please note that the prices given are not necessarily for the specific doll illustrated, but are suggestive of the **type** of doll pictured. Two dolls of the same model, for example, may vary in worth because of condition and the number of replacement parts in each.

Although this guide deals specifically with German, French, and American dolls, two exceptions should be noted: the cloth dolls of Enrico di Scavini ("Lenci") are included because of their worldwide popularity, as are the English wax dolls of the Montanari and Pierotti families.

A Typical Entry

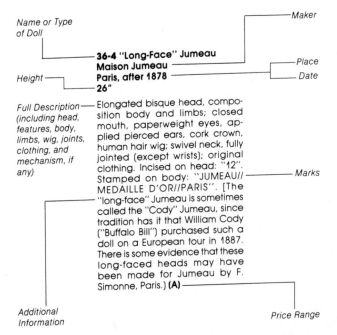

Name or Type of Doll

Height

36-4 "Long-Face" Jumeau
Maison Jumeau
Paris, after 1878
26"

Maker

Place

Date

Full Description (including head, features, body, limbs, wig, joints, clothing, and mechanism, if any) — Elongated bisque head, composition body and limbs; closed mouth, paperweight eyes, applied pierced ears, cork crown, human hair wig; swivel neck, fully jointed (except wrists); original clothing. Incised on head: "12". Stamped on body: "JUMEAU// MEDAILLE D'OR//PARIS". [The "long-face" Jumeau is sometimes called the "Cody" Jumeau, since tradition has it that William Cody ("Buffalo Bill") purchased such a doll on a European tour in 1887. There is some evidence that these long-faced heads may have been made for Jumeau by F. Simonne, Paris.) **(A)**

Marks

Additional Information

Price Range

Introduction

Manufactured dolls and doll parts made during the period 1840 to 1940, including Western European dolls as well as American-made ones, are the focal point of this book. It is these dolls which are the core of the modern doll collector's world. Before this period there were few dolls available which were made on a production basis; after this period there was such a change in the methods of production, sources, and quality of dolls sold worldwide that the years following are the proper subject of another book.

By necessity a work such as this must be selective. Needless to say, not every doll—or even every type of doll—made during the 100-year period can be discussed. In order to talk about dolls in any meaningful way, they must be arranged into categories, and this involves selectivity and exclusion. First, as stated above, this volume concentrates almost entirely on manufactured dolls or "production" dolls—it includes very few completely handmade or one-of-a-kind dolls. And secondly, because of limitations of space and the availability of other works on the subjects, the book does not cover figurines, "piano babies," and other purely decorative objects or two-dimensional paper dolls.

The first dolls—here defined as children's playthings in human form, and not as fetishistic or religious figures—came, presumably, with the first children. There are, at any rate, examples of playthings made especially for children which date back hundreds, if not thousands, of years. Dolls can tell us many things about the societies which produced them. They are indicators, first and most obviously, as to what children did, how they played, and to what purpose. Secondly, dolls serve to convey to us a notion of the values of adults in a society, especially their attitudes toward children—for adults, not children, on the whole, were and continue to be the makers and selectors of dolls. Thirdly, dolls often mirror the development of their prototypes in the real world and help to show us the degree of importance attached by a society to the models after which dolls are patterned. Finally, dolls are in themselves indicia of the technical accomplishments of a society, as are all types of manufactured goods.

The above is true of Western society in the 19th and 20th centuries as well as of earlier and more primitive cultures. Through the dolls which were produced for children, we can see changes and developments not only in the numbers and varieties of playthings with which children were supplied, but also changes in the types of activities in which children were allowed to, encouraged to, and expected to indulge—as well as developments in manufacturing technology in full scale and in miniature. For doll production was, and is, a **business**, designed first and foremost to make money, and its history is as much a study of industrial economics as it is a story of how advances in technology were employed to both create and exploit popular tastes.

In an age in which modern mothers think nothing of their pizza-nourished youngsters stuffing a Brooke Shields doll into a tawdry wardrobe of polyester hot pants and designer jeans, the moral and aesthetic values that earlier parents saw in doll play seem astonishing, if not downright quaint. "Dolls have come to be works of art," observed one writer in 1876, "and mothers select them carefully that they may assist children in getting correct ideas of beauty." Another, referring to young doll lovers as "little mothers," wrote in 1887 that "With a pretty doll, habits of industry, of neatness, and of order can be established. With dolls a little girl can soon learn the art of dressmaking." Yet, in the face of such piety and practicality, there were already people critical of the inventive improvements in dolls brought about by fierce competition within the 19th-century marketplace. That dolls could walk and talk and shut their eyes, and that small fortunes were being spent on the latest Parisian fashions for them, was considered a violation of the "sacred" purpose of dolls for little girls."It can not be said that the modern progress of the doll has an elevating tendency on the young," wrote one critic in 1884. "The primeval object of the doll among the Greeks and Romans—an object persistent through all later history—was early to impart to the mind of the young girl the duties of maternity. The girl with her doll was a mother in embryo, as it were, learning maternal duty and love toward offspring. The doll of to-day is either a source of amusement or inordinate vanity. It has become a mere toy, stripped of its moral teaching." Vanity. An interesting word given our forebears' obsession with dressing dolls in the very latest fashions. How far away in time was the exquisitely-dressed French bisques of the 19th century from Barbie and Brooke Shields, after all?

Doll collecting, then, is many things to many people. It is, no doubt, a nostalgic return for some to the innocent cares of childhood. For others it is a window on the past, a tangible lesson in social history. Nostalgia and history aside, the collectors' interest may be primarily in the aesthetic or decorative aspects of dolls, or in their reflection of the history of technology, or in the prototypes which they represent, or in any number of other things about them. Whatever the motivation, however, there is one rule that applies to all doll collectors: **The wise collector is an educated collector.** The more one knows about dolls, their history and technology, the more difficult it is to be hoodwinked by the myriad hawkers of fakes and reproductions preying on a growing population of collectors. In this, modern collectors are more fortunate than their predecessors of even fifteen years ago who were dependent on the misinformation of books that were more sentimental than accurate.

The publication in 1968 of **The Collector's Encyclopedia of Dolls** by Dorothy, Elizabeth, and Evelyn Coleman rendered obsolete most books published earlier. Thoroughly grounded in historical method, this book is remarkable not only for the astonishing range of its documented findings, but for its candid admission of just how much about dolls remains to be discovered. The book is indispensable, as is Constance Eileen King's **The Collector's History of Dolls.** These two books put to shame the endless round of collectors' books that come pouring off the presses like so much junk food from a supermarket.

It is estimated that there are more than 200 million dolls in the United States alone, most of them now owned by adults. Doll collecting has progressed in the last thirty years from the specialized, if not eccentric, passion of the few to perhaps the largest and fastest-growing hobby in the world. In the face of a diminishing supply of antique dolls and a constantly growing population of doll enthusiasts, one can only underscore the obvious: The wise collector is the educated collector.

Glossary

Applied Ears—Ears attached separately after head is molded; found on quality dolls.

Art Dolls—Dolls designed by artists; less frequently a term used for boudoir-type dolls made for adults.

Bald Heads—Dolls with smooth, fully-molded heads.

Bébé Têteur—Suckling or feeding doll.

Belton Type—French bisque doll with bald head; small holes in crown for stringing or attaching wig.

Bent-limb Body—Baby body in sitting position.

Biedermeier—China doll with a round black spot on pate. Some collectors use the term for any glazed china doll; others for any doll made between 1805 and 1840.

Biskoline—A material similar to celluloid.

Bisque—Unglazed china.

Bonnet Dolls—Dolls with molded hats.

Boudoir Dolls—Lady dolls popular with adults from World War I through the 1930s.

Breast Plate—The shoulders portion of a shoulder head.

Breveté—Patented.

Butterfly Doll—Bonnet doll with hat in shape of butterfly.

Character Doll—Bisque-head doll with realistic expression.

China Head—Doll with glazed porcelain shoulder head.

China Limb—Doll with porcelain lower arms and legs.

Composition—Any mixture of wood or paper pulp with glue as binder.

Crèche Figures—Made for Christmas tableaux.

DEP—Déposé (French) or Deponiert (German); indicates a registered design or trademark.

D.R.G.M.—Deutsches Reichs Gebrauchsmuster (a registered design).

Dutch Dolls—Corruption of Deutsch (German for "German") and used by collectors to mean cheap jointed wooden dolls.

Flange Necks—Found on dolls with cloth bodies; the cloth is sewed over the flange, holding the head on the body and allowing it to rotate.

Flappers—Boudoir dolls with long legs and high-heeled shoes.

Flirting Eyes—Eyes that move from side to side.

French Bisque—Manufacturers' jargon for quality bisque, no matter where it is made.

Frozen Charlottes—Unjointed china dolls of indeterminate sex.

Glaze—The smooth, glossy finish applied to porcelain and earthenware.

Goo-Goo Eyes—Large, round cartoon-like eyes, usually glancing sideways.

Gutta-Percha—The milky substance from certain Malasian trees used in making a rubber-like material.

Grödnertals—Early 19th-century jointed wooden dolls with gilded or yellow combs in hair.

Half Dolls—China head and torso molded in one piece to waist.

Holzmasse—German for "wood pulp."

Hottentots—Black Kewpies.

Intaglio Eyes—Painted dolls' eyes with incised detail.

Jne.—French abbreviation for "Jeune" (Junior).

Mask Face—The printed or molded front of a doll's head that is attached to a stuffed fabric back.

Matryushka—A nest of wooden dolls.

Milliners' Models—A term of doubtful historical accuracy for early 19th-century papier-mâché dolls with molded hair.

Motschmann-Type—Dolls made after 1857 in imitation of oriental dolls, with wax over papier-mâché heads on cloth torsos with composition pelvises.

Molded Yoke—Decoration suggesting collars, etc., on shoulder heads.

Multi-faced Dolls—Several faces selected by a knob at the top of the head.

Needle-molding—Modeling of features on a rag doll by small stitches.

Open-closed Mouths—Mouths modeled in the open position, but having no entry into the head cavity.

Paperweight Eyes—Collectors' jargon for high-quality early flat-backed glass eyes; usually descriptive of French bisques.

Papier-Mâché—Substance made of paper pulp mixed with glue and other materials (e.g., chalk and sand) that hardens after being molded.

Pate—The crown of a doll's head.

Pet Names—China shoulder heads with names ("Helen," "Agnes") embossed on the breast plate.

Pink Lustre—Delicate pink shading on china heads.

Portrait Dolls—Heads modeled on actual persons (Shirley Temple, Jacqueline Kennedy, etc.)

Poupards—Doll's head mounted on a stick, with costume concealing music box or squeaker; also called **folies** or **marottes**.

Poured-Wax—Molded completely from wax.

Pumpkin Heads—Waxed papier-mâché heads with blonde hair, made in shallow two-part molds that result in a flattened appearance; also called "Squash Heads."

Rooted Hair—Hair set, singly or in tufts, in wax (and, later, vinyl) heads.

Schutzmarke—German for "trademark."

S.G.D.G.—Initials for the French words meaning "without government guarantee," i.e., the government does not guarantee that the manufacturer has protected his patent by conducting a patent search.

Shoulder Head—Head and shoulder plate of same substance, generally sewn to body.

Shoulder Plate—Breast plate, which see

Ste.—French abbreviation for Société.

Swivel Necks—Heads that turn in sockets.

Waxed Heads—Heads of papier-mâché or wood coated with wax.

Wire-eyed—Eyes that close by pulling a wire protruding from the side of the doll's body.

Color Key to Dolls

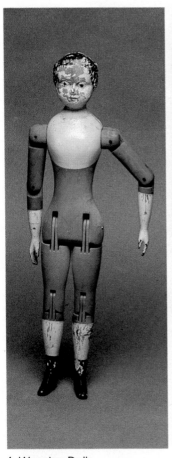

1. Wooden Dolls

2. Rag Dolls

3. Dried Apple Dolls

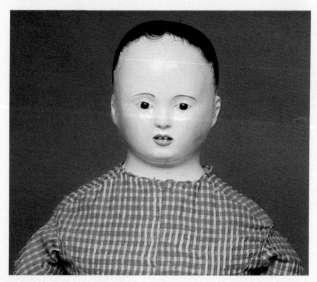

4. Papier-mâché Dolls

5. China Head Dolls

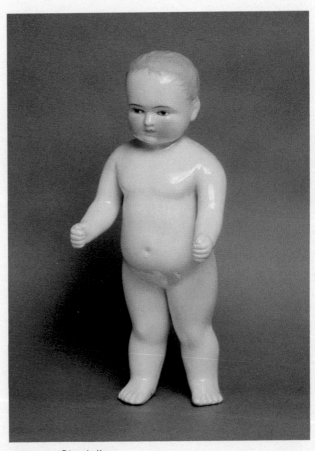

6. Frozen Charlottes

7. China Limb Dolls

8. Leather, Gutta-percha, and Rubber Dolls

9. Wax Dolls

10. Waxed Dolls

11. Bisque Dolls

12. Parian (Untinted Bisque) Dolls

13. Metal Head Dolls

14. Celluloid Dolls

15. Composition Dolls

16. Fashion Dolls

17. Baby Dolls

18. Bye-Lo Babies

19. Lady Dolls

20. Mechanical Dolls

21. Talking Dolls

22. Character Dolls

23. Portrait Dolls

24. Cartoon Character and Storybook Dolls

25. Bonnet Dolls

26. Advertising and Premium Dolls

27. Multi-face, Multi-head, and Topsy-turvy Dolls

28. Kewpies and Other Rose O'Neill Dolls

29. Campbell Kids and Other Grace Drayton Dolls

30. Boudoir Dolls

31. Doll's House Dolls and Other Miniatures

32. Foreign Costume Dolls

33. Black Dolls

34. Novelties

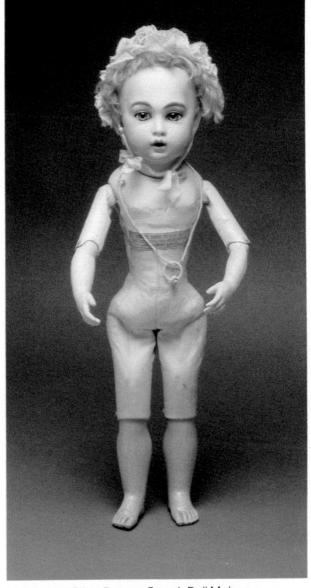

35. Bru and Other Famous French Doll Makers

36. Jumeau

37. Société Française de Fabrication de Bébés et Jouets
and Unis France

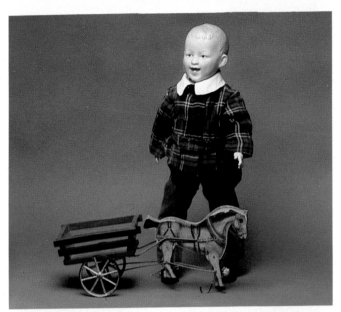

38. Heubach and Other Famous German Doll Makers

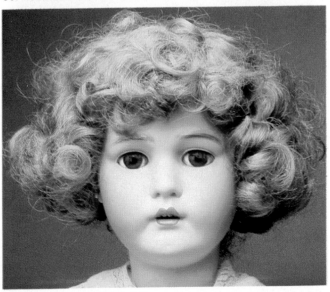

39. Kämmer & Reinhardt

40. Simon & Halbig

41. J. D. Kestner

42. Armand Marseille

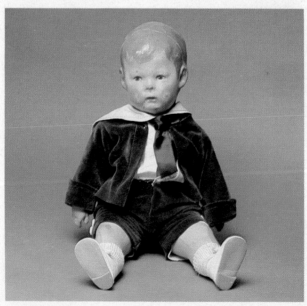

43. Käthe Kruse

44. Ludwig Greiner

45. Fulper Pottery Co.

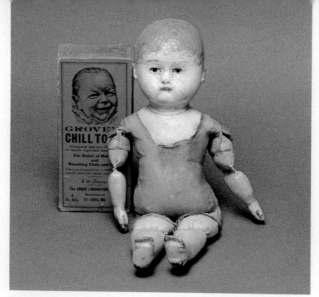

46. Martha J. Chase

47. A. Schoenhut & Co.

48. EFFanBEE

49. Madame Alexander

50. Lenci

I MATERIALS

1 | Wooden Dolls

Wood, a once plentiful and cheap material, was undoubtedly used in making dolls centuries ago, whether by primitively fashioning a plaything from a forked stick with a bit of cloth wrapped around it or by hand-carving an exquisitely realistic crèche figure for a Baroque cathedral (1-1). Because of its hardness, wood has survived the ravages of time far better than wax, cloth, or any other material used in making dolls except clay. For this reason the collector can still readily find surviving examples of an almost astonishing variety of wooden dolls, ranging from the primitive but charming peg-woodens or penny-woodens (incorrectly called "Dutch" dolls), made in the Grödnertal and Berchtesgarden areas of Austria from the 18th through the early 20th centuries (1-2), to the mortise-and-tenon-jointed dolls of Joel Ellis and Mason and Taylor, made in Springfield, Vermont, in the 1870s (1-0, 1-4). Penny-woodens, jointed and fastened together with wooden pegs, possessed flattish faces with sharp noses protruding from round heads, usually painted with black spit curls. Although they were simply constructed, they were sufficiently regarded in their time to have been the favorite playthings of the young Queen Victoria.

Another type of wooden doll, once overlooked but now avidly collected, is the artist's model or wooden lay figure (1-5), whose jointed limbs could be arranged as required and whose use goes back at least as far as the 15th-century painter Albrecht Dürer. The most famous wooden dolls of the 20th century, those produced by A. Schoenhut & Co. of Philadelphia, are discussed and illustrated in section 47.

1-O Joel Ellis Wooden Doll (color plate)
Co-operative Manufacturing Co.
Springfield, Vermont, 1873-74
15"

Wooden doll with mortise-and-tenon joints, pressed and painted features and hair, pewter hands and feet. [Joel Ellis, president of the Co-operative Manufacturing Co., patented this doll in 1873.] **(C)**

1-1 Crèche Figure
Maker unidentified
Spanish, late 17th or early 18th
     century
11"

Carved wood crèche figure, depicting the infant Jesus, with blown-glass eyes, open-closed mouth with three upper teeth, original paint. [Figure is carved from a single block of wood.] **(C)**

1-2 Peg-Jointed Wooden Dolls

Maker and place unidentified
Left: First half of 19th century
Right: Late 19th century
4½" (left), 6" (right)

All-wood dolls; painted features and hair; peg-jointed at shoulders and hips. **(Left, C; right, E)**

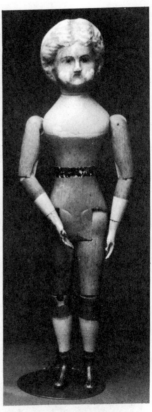

1-3 Wooden Peddlar Doll
Maker unidentified
Probably English, 19th century
11"

Peg-jointed wooden doll; painted features, human hair wig glued over original painted hair; jointed at shoulders and hips. [This is an early wooden doll that was probably dressed later in the century.]
(E)

1-4 Mason and Taylor Doll
D.M. Smith & Co.
Springfield, Vermont, 1881
12"

Composition over wood head, wood body and upper limbs, pewter hands and feet; carved and painted features and hair; jointed at shoulders, elbows, hips, and knees. [Chief improvement of this doll over the Joel Ellis Doll lay in the improved joint which was stronger and more durable. The body of the Mason and Taylor doll is made of soft wood (usually poplar) and was turned from a square block of wood. Legs and arms are made of rock maple or beech, and feet and hands of pewter, usually painted blue. The head is made of a wooden core covered by composition and dipped in flesh-colored paint. Mason and Taylor fingers are practically straight, while Joel Ellis hands are held with fingers curved.] **(D)**

1-5 Artist's Model
Maker and place unidentified
Early 19th century
17"

Carved wood lay doll, jointed with metal pins. Notice jointed waist. [Unlike most wooden dolls of the period, artist's models are anatomically correct in both body proportions and placement of joints.] **(C)**

1-6 Ventriloquist's Dummy
Maker unidentified
American, late 19th century
30" (entire doll), 10" (head alone)

Wooden head, wood-frame chest with straw-stuffed cloth front, cloth arms and legs, wooden hands; portion of face below lower lip made of leather so that mouth can open and close; brown glass eyes set in plaster of Paris, horsehair wig; jointed at shoulders, hips, and knees. [Head is attached to a pole, visible at back, which causes head to swivel. Wire at back operates mouth. A superb example of American folk art.] **(C)**

2 | Rag Dolls

The term "rag doll" is gradually giving way to the more accurate (and less pejorative) term "cloth doll." The common printed cutout "rag" doll, first patented in America in 1886 by Edward S. Peck, was intended as an inexpensive substitute for more costly dolls, thus "democratizing" the manufactured doll by bringing it into the households of even the poorest children. The quality of the textile fabrics that went into their making, however, were in fact anything but rags.

Dolls made of remnants of fabric, stitched together and stuffed, have their origin in ancient times and persisted well into the 20th century, but the homely, yet inevitably charming, cloth dolls cut from manufactured printed patterns and sewn and stuffed at home by the child or her mother, provide the majority of examples available to the collector today. These machine-printed dolls range in quality from the relatively realistic six-piece patterns of Ida Gutsell (2-3) to the more common two-dimensional products of the Art Fabric Mills (2-5). The cheapness of the lithographed cutout rag doll led to its frequent use as early 20th-century advertising premiums, and many examples of this type—now a specialized collector's area in itself—are shown in section 26.

The very sophisticated cloth dolls of Margarete Steiff (38-15), Martha Chase (section 46), Käthe Kruse (section 43), and Lenci (section 50) are treated elsewhere in this book.

2-0 Rag Doll (color plate)
Maker unidentified
American, c. 1900
26"

Cutout printed cloth doll with lithographed face, underwear, high-button shoes, and stockings. Unmarked. **(E)**

2-1 Rag Doll
Maker and place unidentified
c. 1860-70
24" (entire doll)
6½" (shoulder head)

Stockinet-cloth shoulder head reinforced with metal around the shoulder edge, cloth body and limbs, molded and painted features and hair; jointed at shoulders, hips, and knees. **(E)**

2-2 Sheppard Rag Doll
J.B. Sheppard & Co.
Philadelphia, Pennsylvania
c. 1890
21"

Rag doll; features, hands, and feet oil-painted and needle molded; jointed at shoulders and hips. Unmarked, but typical of Sheppard output. [These dolls are sometimes called "Philadelphia Babies."] **(D)**

2-3 Rag Doll
Patented by Ida Gutsell
Cocheco Manufacturing Co.
American, 1893
16"

Cutout printed cloth doll with brown lithographed features, hair, and underclothing; underclothing outlined in red; original brown suit. [Doll was also available in blue suit. Gutsell's patent called for a realistic doll with a seam down the center of the face. Lawrence & Co. of Boston, Massachusetts, also produced the cloth patterns for Gutsell dolls.] **(E)**

2-4 Brownie (John Bull)
Arnold Print Works
North Adams, Massachusetts
c. 1892
7"

Two-piece printed rag doll, sewn
and stuffed. Printed on rear of
right foot: "Copyrighted 1892//by
PALMER COX". [Brownie patterns
were printed twelve to a yard of
fabric, and all twelve sold for
about 20¢. Each had a front and a
back and were to be sewn and
stuffed by the buyer. Palmer Cox
was the creator of the Brownie
characters.] **(E)**

2-5 Art Fabric "Life Size" Doll
        (Merrie Marie)
Art Fabric Mills
Distributed by Selchow & Righter
New York City, c. 1900
25"

Cutout printed rag doll with lithographed red hair ribbon and
stockings, and high black boots.
Printed on bottom of right foot:
"ART FABRIC MILLS//NEW YORK//
Patented Feb. 13th 1900". [Edgar
G. Newell, president of Art Fabric
Mills, patented an infant-sized doll
to be dressed by children in cast-
off baby clothes; he called his
product "The Life Size Doll."] **(E)**

2-6 Brückner Rag Doll
Albert Brückner
Jersey City, New Jersey, c. 1901
Originally 14½"

Lithographed rag doll, jointed at shoulders. Stamped on neck: "PAT'D. JULY 8TH 1901." [This doll was originally half of a two-headed topsy-turvy doll; it was attached to the toy illustrated sometime in the 1930s.] **(E)**

2-7 Raggedy Ann and Andy
Designed by John B. Gruelle
Molly' Es Doll Outfitters, Inc.
Philadelphia, Pennsylvania, 1930s
32" (Raggedy Ann), 31" (Andy)

Rag dolls jointed at shoulders, elbows, hips, and knees; button eyes
and yarn hair. **(Each, F)**

2-8 Henry VIII and Anne Boleyn
Liberty of London
London, 1930s
10" (each)

Cloth dolls dressed in remnants of the expensive fabrics sold by Liberty;
hand-painted features. [The complete set includes the additional five
wives of Henry VIII: Catherine of Aragon, Jane Seymour, Anne of
Cleves, Catherine Howard, and Catherine Parr, each 10" high and
each expensively dressed.] **(Each E)**

3 | Dried Apple Dolls

No one who enjoys the aesthetic pleasures of doll collecting can ignore an even deeper impulse underlying an interest in dolls: Throughout history the need of the child (and of many adults) to transfer love to an inanimate object in human form has transcended time, place, and regional culture. The survival in modern times of primitive means of producing dolls, especially in rural areas, attests to the universality of this love. Dolls have been made (and continue to be made) from bones, corncobs, and cornhusks, and the modern collector should have at least a few examples of such primitive doll making as a humble reminder of mankind's essential need for the affecting comfort of dolls.

The recent craft revival has witnessed a renewed interest in dolls made from dried apples. Although the form is indigenous to the mountain regions of North Carolina, it was hardly unknown in 19th-century England, where it was particularly popular for making the withered crone-like faces of peddlar dolls. An apple placed on a stick would be carved to suggest the features of a face. After dipping in vinegar, the head would be allowed to dry naturally, forming, generally, an old, wrinkled, rather homely visage. Although dried apple heads are still best suited for representing old people (3-1, 3-2), they are adaptable to many imaginative uses (3-3) and are not entirely without their own peculiar charm.

3-O Dried-Apple Doll (color plate)
Maker unidentified
American, 20th century
9"

Dried-apple head on cloth body with cloth over wire limbs. **(F)**

3-1 Dried-Apple Doll
Maker unidentified
American, 20th century
9"

Dried apple head on cloth body with cloth over wire limbs. **(F)**

3-2 Dried-Apple Doll
Maker unidentified
American, 20th century
9"

Dried apple head on cloth body with cloth over wire limbs. **(F)**

3-3 Dried-Apple Raggedy Ann and Andy
Plostina Brady
Benton, Pennsylvania, contemporary
6" (each)

Dried-apple heads on cloth bodies; painted features, yarn hair. **(Pair, F)**

4 | Papier-mâché Dolls

Papier-mâché is a type of composition described in a 19th-century
dictionary as "a tough plastic material made from paper pulp containing an admixture of size, paste, oil, resin, or other substances or
from sheets of paper glued and pressed together." Although known
to have been used in the making of dolls' heads from at least the 16th
century, and readily employed in the production of French and German handmade toys throughout the 18th century, papier-mâché
came into its own as a major material of doll making only after the
means of mass producing dolls' heads in molds by a pressure process
was perfected. It is said that the process, introduced to Germany by
Friedrich Müller who had learned it from a French soldier, was the
basis for the great German doll industry that flourished through the
19th century and well into the 20th.

Although the manufacture of papier-mâché heads reached its zenith in the 1850s, it had already created a new type of doll three decades earlier. The so-called "milliner's model" (see 16-1) featured a papier-mâché head on a kid body with wooden limbs. Papier-mâché heads were produced throughout the 19th century in France, Germany, and America, the majority of extant examples being unmarked. Later 19th-century heads have been found with such marks as the trademark "Holz Masse" (Otto and Kuno Dressel) and "M & S Superior" (see 4-5). The American papier-mâché heads made by Ludwig Greiner of Philadelphia are treated in section 44.

4-0 Papier-mâché Doll (color plate)
Maker unidentified
French, c. 1810
26" (entire doll), 6½" (shoulder head)

Papier-mâché head, pink kid body and limbs; open mouth with four bamboo teeth, brown glass pupil-less eyes, molded features, painted hair; jointed at shoulders and hips; original clothing. Unmarked. [Doll is believed to be Alsatian.] **(C)**

4-1 Early Papier-mâché Doll
Maker unidentified
French, c. 1820
20" (entire doll), 5½" (shoulder head)

Papier-mâché shoulder head; hand-sewn cloth body with kid limbs; molded and painted features, pupil-less enamel eyes, solid dome painted black with a slit in middle to fasten wig, original human hair wig in tiny braids indicates early origin. **(C)**

4-2 Papier-mâché Shoulder Head (left)
Maker unidentified
German, mid-19th century
14" (entire doll)
4½" (shoulder head)

Papier-mâché shoulder head on straw-filled cloth body with bisque lower limbs; closed mouth, glass sleeping eyes, wig missing; jointed at shoulders and hips. **(E)**

Papier-mâché Shoulder Head (right)
Maker unidentified
German, mid-19th century
18" (entire doll)
5" (shoulder head)

Papier-mâché shoulder head on straw-filled cloth body with bisque lower limbs; closed mouth, glass eyes, pierced ears, human hair wig; jointed at shoulders and hips. **(E)**

4-3 Pre-Greiner Papier-mâché Doll
Maker unidentified
American, mid-19th century
32" (entire doll)
8½" (shoulder head)

Papier-mâché shoulder head, cloth body and legs, kid arms; molded and painted features and hair, glass pupil-less eyes; jointed at shoulders, hips, and knees. **(D)**

4-4 Papier-mâché Dolls
Maker and place unidentified
Mid-19th century
11″ (left), 9″ (right)

Papier-mâché shoulder heads on cloth bodies, molded and painted features and molded blonde hair, glass eyes; jointed at shoulders and hips. **(Each, E)**

4-5 Superior Papier-mâché Doll
Probably Müller & Strassburger
Sonneberg, Thür., c. 1870
30" (entire doll)
8" (shoulder head)

Papier-mâché shoulder head, cloth body and legs; kid arms; molded and painted features and hair; jointed at shoulders, hips, and knees. Label on base of breast plate: "M&S//Superior// 2015". **(D)**

4-6 Carton Moulé
Maker unidentified
French, late 19th century
21"

Papier-mâché head, body, and limbs; molded and painted features and blue-painted clothing; swivel neck, jointed at shoulders. [Dressed in either blue or pink, dolls like this are believed to have been given to expectant mothers to make their wish for a male or female child come true.] **(D)**

5 | China Head Dolls

China dolls should be properly called "glazed porcelain dolls," for there really is no substance known to ceramics manufacturers as "china." Still, there is a logical wisdom to this popular term used by doll collectors everywhere to distinguish between heads made from glazed porcelain (china) and unglazed porcelain (bisque). Perhaps the best descriptive definition of china head dolls is that of Catherine Christopher in **The Complete Book of Doll Making and Collecting:** "There are three grades of china: blue, white, creamy white, and flesh-toned, the latter being known as pink luster. China heads are modeled in clay, glazed, and then fired at a high temperature in a kiln. The all-over coloring and the evenness of its tone is indicative of the grade of the finished article: blue white being most common, the creamy being better, and the so-called pink luster the best. Although we call them dolls, we are actually discussing and defining doll heads. Contrary to other material classifications (wood, rag, etc.), so-called china dolls had bodies made of cloth or kid. Arms and legs may be of matching china [see section 7] or may be of the body material. There is only one all-china doll. It is called a Frozen Charlotte [see section 6]."

Because china dolls were produced in abundance for more than eighty years, a good number survive today that defy artificial systems of classification devised by modern collectors. Almost all china dolls made before 1891 (the vast majority) were unmarked, a situation that has invited all sorts of undocumented methods of classification and dating. Realizing that a great deal of research remains to be done before any reliable system can be established, the collector would be wise to dismiss such classifications as "Jennie Lind," "Adelina Patti," "Mary Todd Lincoln," and "Queen Victoria," since it is doubtful that these historic personages were the actual models for particular types of heads. Nonetheless, it is obvious that china heads can be grouped according to hair style, even though hair style alone is a less than perfect way of dating a doll with any accuracy; the same mold could easily have been used for decades.

Except for the tenuous clues provided by hair styles (the best guide is in the indispensable **Collector's Encyclopedia of Dolls**), it remains difficult to approximate the age of china dolls. There are additional signposts, however. The older shoulder heads were modeled with a deep breast plate so that the doll could be dressed in the low-cut gowns popular in the first part of the 19th century. As a rule, then, the breast plate became shorter as the century progressed. In addition, it is believed that china dolls with oval-shaped painted eyes are older than those with round eyes. Short, thick necks are characteristic of shoulder heads made in the late 19th and early 20th centuries, just as the so-called "low-brow," with painted hair covering the forehead, dates from the same period.

Given the large numbers of china head dolls on the market today, rareness is generally determined by quality of porcelain, uniqueness of hair style, and the fineness of brush strokes; in addition, blonde china heads are far less common than black-haired dolls and swivel-necked china heads are much more uncommon than one-piece shoulder heads.

5-O China-Head Doll (color plate, left)
Maker unidentified
German, mid-19th century
24" (entire doll), 7" (shoulder head)

Flesh-tinted china shoulder head on cloth body with leather arms and cloth legs; molded and painted features and hair, brown eyes; hair style and original clothing suggest origin in mid-19th century. **(D)**

Blonde China-Head Boy (color plate, right)
Maker unidentified
German, late 19th century
23"

China shoulder head on cloth body with leather arms and cloth legs; molded and painted features and hair; contemporary clothing. **(D)**

5-1 China Shoulder Head
Maker unknown
German, c. mid-19th century
7"

China shoulder head; molded and painted features and hair, lips painted to suggest open-closed mouth. Marked inside breast plate: "13". [Holes at base show method of attaching shoulder head to body.] **(E)**

5-2 China Head
Maker unidentified
German, first half of 19th century
9½" (shoulder head alone)

China shoulder head with molded and painted features and hair; hair style, puffed at sides and twisted into a wreath at back, suggests origin in 1840s or '50s. **(D)**

5-3 Brown-Eyed China Head
Maker unidentified
German, mid-19th century
23" (entire doll)
7" (shoulder head)

China shoulder head on cloth body stuffed with straw, leather arms; molded and painted features and hair; brown eyes with

painted lower lashes; hair style typical of dolls exhibited in mid-century. **(C)**

**5-4 China Head
Maker unidentified
German, 19th century
22" (entire doll), 5" (shoulder head)**

China shoulder head on cloth body with leather arms and cloth legs; molded and painted features and hair; hair style and original clothing suggest origin in 1860s. **(D)**

5-5 China-Head Doll

Maker unidentified
German, 19th century
25" (entire doll), 7½" (shoulder head)

China shoulder head on cloth body with kid arms and cloth legs; molded and painted features and hair; hair style suggests origin in 1860s. **(D)**

5-6 "Greiner" China-Head Doll
Maker unidentified
German, mid-19th century
14" (entire doll)
4¼" (shoulder head)

China shoulder head, cloth body with leather arms and cloth legs; molded and painted features and hair; hair style suggests origin in 1850s or '60s. [Because their hair styles resemble that of Greiner papier-mâché dolls, such china dolls are sometimes called "China Greiners" by collectors.] **(D)**

5-7 China-Head Doll
Maker unidentified
German, late 19th century
36" (entire doll)
8" (shoulder head)

China shoulder head on cloth body with kid forearms; molded and painted features and hair. **(D)**

5-8 China Head with Pierced Ears
Maker unidentified
German, second half of 19th
century
19"

China shoulder head on cloth
body with leather arms and cloth
legs; molded and painted features and hair; pierced ears; hair
style suggests origin in 1870s. **(D)**

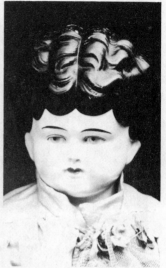

5-9 "Low-Brow" China Head
Maker and place unidentified
c. 1899
25"

China shoulder head on cloth
body with kid arms and cloth legs.
("Low-brow" hair style was produced from c. 1880-c. 1914, although original clothing suggests
origin at turn of century.) **(E)**

5-10 Pet-Name China Doll
Butler Bros.
Sonneberg, Thür., c. 1905
17" (entire doll)
4" (shoulder head)

China shoulder head on cloth
body; molded and painted features and hair, "low-brow" hair
style, molded and painted boots;
gilt band around collar; gilt over
embossed name, "BERTHA", on
breast plate. **(E)**

6 | Frozen Charlottes

Frozen Charlottes are one-piece molded porcelain dolls that are completely unjointed. Known also as pillar dolls, solid-china dolls, or bathing babies, they were produced either glazed or unglazed (although the glazed were far more common) and in a variety of grades and sizes. Most Frozen Charlottes are chubby nudes of indeterminate sex with clenched fists and bent elbows. The wide variety of hair styles would suggest that the dolls were intended to be female, although it should be remembered that through most of the 19th century male and female children were dressed and coiffed identically. Modern doll collectors who insist that they know a male Frozen Charlotte when they see one call such dolls "Frozen Charlies." Pillar dolls range in size from one to over eighteen inches high and occasionally wear molded bonnets or hair ribbons, despite their nudity. Of the several explanations of the term "Frozen Charlotte," the most plausible derives from a Civil War ballad about "fair Charlotte," who, eager to be wooed by her suitor one winter's night, went out into the Vermont cold wearing only a silken cloak and promptly froze to death.

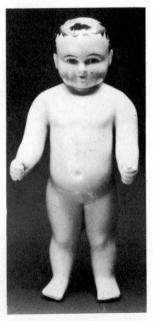

6-0 Frozen Charlie (color plate)
Maker unidentified
German, early 20th century
15"

Glazed china pillar doll, delicately flesh-tinted head, painted blue eyes, fine brush marks around the blonde hair line. [Male Frozen Charlottes are sometimes called "Frozen Charlies" by collectors.] **(D)**

6-1 Frozen Charlie
Maker unidentified
German, early 20th century
12"

Glazed china pillar doll, flesh-tinted head, painted brown eyes, fine brush marks around black hairline; long torso and short neck. **(D)**

6-2 Frozen Charlotte
Maker unidentified
German, early 20th century
4½"

Glazed china pillar doll, pink-lustre head, molded and painted features and hair. **(D)**

6-3 Miniature Frozen Charlottes
Maker unidentified
German, late 19th-early 20th centuries
Range in size from 3" to 6"

(Each, F)

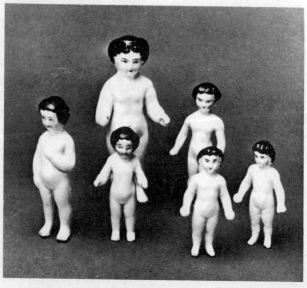

7 | China Limb Dolls

As the name itself suggests, china-limb dolls are china-head dolls with lower arms and legs of porcelain. Originally found on jointed wooden bodies in the middle of the 19th century, china limbs later appeared on both jointed and unjointed cloth bodies. China legs usually had molded and painted shoes and stockings, with flat heels in vogue before 1870 and high heels becoming more pronounced as the century progressed. Legs with elaborate garters are considered to be of late origin.

It is often suggested that china-limb dolls were commercially assembled and sold intact, but this is far from established fact. Like the simple china-head doll, those with china limbs could be bought in individual parts at country stores and assembled at home. The grotesque proportions of some china-limb dolls and the poor stitching frequently found suggest, in fact, that children themselves often assembled these dolls. In this regard, the sewing of the body can sometimes help to approximate the age of china dolls: the sewing machine was not in general use until 1870 or so. But even after 1890, when most manufacturers had abandoned hand-sewing, parts could still be purchased separately for hand-stitching at home.

7-O Dolley Madison-type China-Limb Doll (color plate, left)
Maker unidentified
Possibly German, c. 1880
23"

China shoulder head, cloth body with china arms and legs, painted black boots with red buttons; painted features, molded and painted black hair with blue hair ribbon. [Collectors occasionally call this type of head "Dolley Madison," although there is no evidence that a portrait of Mrs. Madison served as the model for the head.] **(D)**

China-Limb Boy (color plate, right)
Maker unidentifed
German, late 19th century
22"

China shoulder head on cloth body with china arms and cloth legs; molded and painted features and hair; original clothing. **(D)**

7-1 China-Limb Boy
Maker unidentified
German, late 19th century
15½"

China shoulder head on cloth body with china limbs; molded and painted features and hair, with hair style appropriate for a young boy or girl. **(E)**

7-2 Blonde China-Limb Doll
Maker and place unidentified
Mid-19th century
13"

Glazed china shoulder head on cloth body with china arms; molded and painted features and hair, rare hair style, pierced ears; jointed at shoulders and hips. **(D)**

7-3 China-Limb Dolls
Maker unidentified
German, 19th century
Left: 10" (entire doll, 3" (shoulder head)
Right: 8" (entire doll), 2" shoulder head)

China shoulder heads on cloth

bodies with china forearms and legs with boots; molded and painted features and hair; jointed at shoulders and hips. [Doll at right, a "lowbrow," and certainly later than doll at left, has gilded laces on boots. Hair style of doll at left and original clothing suggests origin in 1860s.] **(Each, E)**

7-4 China-Limb Dolls
Makers unidentified
German, early 20th century
Left: 18" (entire doll), 4½" (shoulder head)
Right: 16½" (entire doll), 4½" (shoulder head)

China shoulder heads on cloth bodies with china arms and legs; molded and painted features and hair (notice blonde hair on right), jointed at shoulders and hips. ["Lowbrow" hair styles indicate origin in late 19th or early 20th centuries.] **(Each, E)**

**7-5 Modern China-Limb Doll
Emma C. Clear
Los Angeles, California, 1947
18½"**

Pink-tinted china shoulder head on cloth body with china lower limbs and boots; molded and painted features and hair; jointed at shoulders, hips, and knees. Incised on back of breast plate: "47 Clear [in script]". **(D)**

8 | Leather, Gutta-percha, and Rubber Dolls

Of the many materials used in making dolls' heads, perhaps the most uncommon is leather. Although kid bodies were popular throughout the 19th century and as late as the 1930s, few realize that heads, as well as entire dolls, were made of kid and other leathers. All-leather dolls were advertised in Philadelphia as early as 1822 and kid heads on wooden bodies have been dated from the 1840s. In 1866 Pierre Clement patented an all-leather doll in France at the same time that Franklin Darrow was issued a U.S. patent for a leather doll's head. Other all-leather dolls were patented in America in 1903, with patents for leather heads granted as late as 1917. The kid doll illustrated in 8-0 is entirely handmade, its very homeliness an integral part of its engaging charm.

Gutta-percha is a substance made from the sap of Maylasian trees. Although used by doll makers as early as the 1820s, it did not come into regular use until the 1850s when the new industrial age had made possible the search for an indestructible material for making dolls. As Constance King writes in her exemplary **Collector's History of Dolls:** "It is extremely difficult, except by chemical analysis, to distinguish between rubber and gutta-percha, as both harden similarly and crack with time. The tendency for the color to flake away is also common to both materials. The distinction is further complicated by the fact that a combination of the two was sometimes used. Gutta-percha is made malleable by immersion in hot steam or water, which enables it to be molded when it reaches a temperature of 190° F." Because of its extreme brittleness, examples of gutta-percha dolls are not common. Among the makers who used gutta-percha dolls were Richard A. Brooman, Mlle. Calixte Huret, Lang & Co., and Henry Payne.

Although rubber had been used for making dolls for centuries, it was only after Charles Goodyear developed the process of vulcanizing rubber in 1851 that rubber came into its own as an acceptable substance for doll making. The Goodyear Company, in fact, produced a line of rubber dolls, which are rare collector's items today. Rubber dolls were never considered to be a particularly fine form of the doll maker's art, and most German manufacturers snubbed the substance and thought it typical of English and American vulgarity. Like gutta-percha, rubber cracks and chips with age, and fine examples from the past are not common. One use to which rubber dolls were put was the development of the "drink and wet" baby (see 48-5), in which the doll appeared to wet its diapers at a place that was anatomically incorrect. Apparently, parents did not wish their children's playthings to be **too** realistic!

8-0 Kid-Head Doll (color plate)
Maker unidentified
American, c. 1840
19½"

Kid head, sawdust-filled cloth body and limbs; needle-molded features, shoe-button eyes; jointed at shoulders, hips, and knees. [A fine example of an entirely handmade doll.] **(E)**

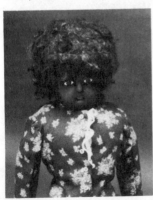

8-1 Gutta-percha Doll
Maker and place unknown
1860s
21" (entire doll)
6" (shoulder head)

Gutta-percha shoulder head on replacement cloth body with gutta-percha arms and lower legs; molded and painted features, horsehair wig; molded and painted boots; jointed at shoulders, hips, and knees; contemporary clothing. **(D)**

8-2 Crèche Figures
Maker unidentified
Probably Italian, 19th century
11½" (each)

Gutta-percha heads and hands on wooden bodies; carved and painted features and hair; unjointed. **(Each, D)**

8-3 Crying Rubber Doll
Maker and place unidentified
Early 20th century
20"

Rubber head on cloth body with rubber forearms and lower legs; open-closed mouth with tongue, molded features and hair; molded and painted eyes. **(F)**

8-4 Little Natalia
The Sun Rubber Co.
Barberton, Ohio, 1935
8"

All-rubber doll with molded and painted features. Incised on back of body: "Little Natalia [in script]". Incised on bottom of right foot: "THE//SUN//RUBBER CO.//BARBERTON//OHIO U.S.A.". [Despite its appearance, this doll was modeled on the little girl who won the New York *Daily News* first "Beautiful Child" contest. A good example of how rubber dries and deteriorates over time.] **(F)**

9 | Wax Dolls

There are essentially three types of wax dolls: solid wax, poured wax, and wax over a composition, wood, or metal foundation. Until 1850 wax heads were literally modeled by hand, and these are called "solid-wax heads." After 1850 molds were used in industrial production so that the wax could be poured, and heads produced this way became known as "poured-wax heads." The third type, wax over composition (known to collectors as "waxed dolls") is the subject of section 10.

In all three types, except for wax baby dolls, the head is usually the only part made of wax, the bodies almost always made of cloth or kid. Dolls with wax legs and feet are relatively rare; less rare are dolls with wax hands. Baby dolls were frequently made entirely of wax and range from exquisite figures with glass eyes (9-1) to crudely modeled "penny dolls," so-called because they were sold for that cheap sum in the 19th century. The wax dolls most prized by collectors, however, are the large lady dolls made by the firms of Montanari (9-0) and Pierotti, both of which, like several other specialists in wax (notably Madame Tussaud), flourished in 19th-century London. These poured-wax dolls, executed with great care and workmanship, feature human hair inserted strand by strand in the wax scalp and the best imported German glass eyes. (Less expensive models had their hair inserted through a center slit in the head.)

Although wax dolls were made by the ancient Greeks and flowered as great religious art in the 17th and 18th centuries, their heyday for modern collectors was the last half of the 19th century. Wax dolls are not as popular with collectors as bisques, of course, but one should remember for the future that surviving examples are much rarer and, therefore, potentially more valuable.

9-O Wax Doll (color plate)
Mme. Augusta Montanari
London, c. 1855
22"

Wax shoulder head, cloth body with wax arms and lower legs; glass eyes, human hair inserted individually in small groups; jointed at shoulders and above knees. Marked on body: "[in script] Montanari//180 Soho Bazaar//London". **(C)**

9-1 Poured-Wax Crèche Figure
Attributed to Henry Pierotti
London, c. 1860s
18"

Poured-wax figure with glass eyes, replacement human hair wig. [Pierotti's most expensive wax dolls usually had inserted hair.] **(D)**

9-2 Wire-Eyed Wax Doll (left)
Maker unidentified
Possibly England, early 19th century
16" (entire doll), 4" (shoulder head)

Wax shoulder head on cloth body; molded features, glass eyes, human hair wig; jointed at shoulders and hips. [Eyes move by a wire at the waist of the doll.] **(C)**

Wax Doll (right)
Maker and place unidentified
Late 18th or early 19th century
15" (entire doll), 5" (shoulder head)

Wax shoulder head on cloth body; molded features, glass pupil-less eyes, human hair wig; jointed at shoulders and hips. **(C)**

9-3 Wire-Eyed Wax Doll
Maker unidentified
Possibly England, mid-19th century
28½" (entire doll), 8" (shoulder head)

Poured-wax shoulder head, cloth body with kid hands; molded and

painted features, brown glass eyes, human hair wig; jointed at shoulders, hips, and knees. [Wire at waist causes eyes to open and close.]
(B)

9-4 Wax Dolls

Makers and place unidentified
Late 19th century
Left: 23" (entire doll), 7" (shoulder head)
Right: 27" (entire doll), 8" (shoulder head)

Left: Wax shoulder head on cloth body with composition forearms and wooden legs and boots; molded features, sleeping glass eyes, human hair wig; jointed at shoulders and hips. [This doll has a particularly deep shoulder plate.] **(D)**

Right: Wax shoulder head on cloth body with kid hands; open mouth with four upper teeth, brown glass sleeping eyes, human hair wig; jointed at shoulders and hips. [Very deep shoulder plate.] **(D)**

9-5 Wax Doll
Maker unidentified
Possibly English, 19th century
22" (entire doll), 6" (shoulder head)

Poured-wax shoulder head on sawdust-filled cloth body with wax arms and lower legs; closed mouth, glass sleeping eyes, human hair wig; jointed at shoulders, hips, and knees. [Doll may have been made by the Montanari family.] **(D)**

9-6 Wax Doll
Maker unidentified
Probably English, 19th century
26" (entire doll)
7" (shoulder head)

Wax shoulder head on cloth body with blue kid hands; closed mouth, glass pupil-less eyes, human hair wig; jointed at shoulders and hips. **(C)**

9-7 Poured-Wax Baby
Carmelite Nuns
French, 20th century
16"

Poured-wax head, body, and limbs; molded and painted features, inserted hair. **(D)**

10 | Waxed Dolls

Although almost every kind of doll-making material has been covered with wax to improve appearance, the type of waxed doll most commonly available to the collector has a head made of wax over papier-mâché on a straw-filled cloth body. The earliest examples of these dolls, made in the first half of the 19th century, have hair set into a slit in the head and large, black (all-pupil) eyes. Later waxed dolls, made in great abundance after 1850, have wigs attached by glue and higher-quality eyes. Of these later dolls, many have waxed composition limbs which give them proportions far more realistic than the earlier leather arms. The features on early waxed dolls were painted on the faces before they were covered with wax; later the features were painted on the wax itself.

Looking very much like odd yellow-colored Hubbard squash, "pumpkin head" waxed dolls have blonde ornately-molded upswept hair and round, moon-shaped faces that are very narrow from back to front. These appealingly homely dolls are actually the direct result of early industrial cost-saving techniques: The shallow heads require only a two-part mold, less drying time than other papier-mâché shells, and—with color applied to the papier-mâché itself—only an ordinary white wax to cover both hair and face, thus saving several finishing processes.

10-0 Waxed Dolls (color plate)
Makers unidentified
German, 19th century
11" (left), 24" (right)

Wax over papier-mâché shoulder head on straw-filled cloth bodies with papier-mâché lower limbs; molded and painted features, glass pupil-less eyes, human hair wigs; jointed at shoulders, hips, and knees. **(Each, D)**

10-1 Waxed Shoulder-Head Doll
Attributed to Schmitt & Fils
Paris, c. 1885
23" (entire doll)
6" (shoulder head)

Wax over composition shoulder head, cloth body and legs, kid forearms; turned head, closed mouth, brown glass eyes; jointed at shoulders, hips, and knees. [Unmarked, but bears a striking resemblance to shoulder heads made by Schmitt & Fils.] **(C)**

10-2 Pumpkin-Head Waxed Doll
Maker unidentified
German, 19th century
16½" (entire doll)
4½" (shoulder head)

Wax over papier-mâché shoulder
head on straw-filled cloth body
with wooden arms and legs; molded and painted features and
blonde hair, glass eyes; orange
painted boots; original clothing.
(D)

10-3 Pumpkin Heads
Makers unidentified
German, 19th century
Shoulder heads, from left to right, 6", 4¼", 4¼"

Wax over papier-mâché shoulder heads on cloth bodies. Doll at right
has composition arms, legs, and boots, and pierced ears. Dolls on left
have wooden arms, legs, and boots. All three have pupil-less glass
eyes and molded pompadour hair styles with hair ribbons. **(Each, D)**

10-4 Pumpkin-Head Waxed Doll
Maker unidentified
German, 19th century
24" (entire doll)
9" (shoulder head)

Wax over papier-mâché shoulder head on straw-filled cloth body with papier-mâché arms and legs; glass eyes, molded and painted features and blonde hair; molded and painted high-button shoes; original clothing. **(D)**

11 | Bisque Dolls

The history of the bisque doll parallels the history of the china-head doll for bisque is merely unglazed "china." "The main difference between china and bisque," Catherine Christopher writes, "is easily recognized; china has a high glaze while bisque has a dull, soft-looking surface. The color of china heads is controlled by the basic color of the clay and the tone of the glaze which is applied before firing. The flesh color of bisque is controlled by the artistry and color sense of the manufacturer since it is an artificial color also applied to the clay before firing. This color, really a glaze, sinks into the porous surface of the clay and is fused therein, making it permanent. The so-called 'French Bisque' has a faint flesh color ground into the clay before modeling and firing. This is the finest bisque of all."

Throughout the 19th century and well into the 20th, bisque heads—made primarily in Germany and France, although some were manufactured in England and the United States because of the disruption of trade during World War I—were used on cloth, kid, and composition bodies. Sometimes, bisque hands and feet were made to match the heads, although it was more usual to have the feet of kid or the body material. Both the shoulder head and swivel neck styles were used for bisque heads.

The bisque dolls in this section can only suggest the great variety available to the collector. Almost 200 additional examples are illustrated in the sections composing Parts II and III of this book.

11-O Bisque-Head Boy (color plate, left)
Unis France
Paris, c. 1922
24"

Bisque head, composition body and limbs; open mouth with four upper teeth, glass sleeping eyes with lashes, molded eyebrows, human hair wig. Incised on back of head: "UNIS//FRANCE [within oval]//71 149//301". **(C)**

Bisque-Head Girl (color plate, right)
Armand Marseille
Köppelsdorf, Thür., early 20th century
21"

Bisque head, composition body and limbs; open mouth with four upper teeth, brown glass eyes, molded eyebrows, human hair wig; swivel neck, fully jointed. Incised on back of head: "Germany//Armand Marseille//390//DRGM//A & M". **(D)**

11-1 Turned-Head Bisque Doll
Maker unidentified
Probably German, second half of 19th century
19" (entire doll)
5½" (shoulder head)

Bisque shoulder head on kid body with bisque forearms; open mouth with four upper teeth, glass sleeping eyes, human hair wig; jointed at shoulders, hips, and knees. Unmarked. [Doll's head is permanently turned to right on breast plate.] **(D)**

11-2 Bisque Shoulder-Head Peddlar Doll
**Maker and place unidentified
19th century
13"**

Bisque shoulder head on paper cone-shaped body, cloth arms; painted eyes, molded and painted hair; original clothing; original notions in wire and woven-wool basket. [Note the fine quality bisque, rare in this type of doll.] **(D)**

11-3

11-3 "Belton-Type" Bisque Doll
**Maker unidentified
Probably French, late 19th century
26"**

Bisque head, composition body and limbs; closed mouth, paperweight eyes, pierced ears, human hair wig; swivel neck, fully jointed (except wrists). Head incised: "183". [Collectors call a bald head with from one to three small holes in the crown for fastening the wig or stringing the doll a "Belton-type" doll. Despite the term, the doll has no historical connection with dolls made by Belton & Jumeau.] **(C)**

11-4 Closed-Mouth Bisque Shoulder Head

11-5

**Probably Simon & Halbig
Gräfenhain, Thür., c. 1900 or
    earlier
21" (entire doll)
5" (shoulder head)**

Bisque shoulder head on kid body
with bisque forearms; closed
mouth, glass eyes, human hair
wig; jointed at shoulders and hips.
Incised on back of shoulder plate:
"309-6" [Photographed without
wig to show solid dome with single
hole for affixing wig. Head is probably an early Simon & Halbig.] **(D)**

**11-5 Bisque Shoulder-Head Doll
Maker and place unidentified
c. 1893
15½"**

Bisque shoulder head on kid body
with bisque forearms; closed
mouth, molded and painted features and hair; jointed at shoulders, hips, knees. [This doll is re-
puted to have been purchased at
the Columbian Exposition of
1893.] **(D)**

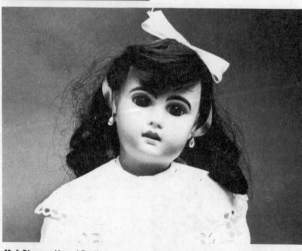

11-6 Bisque-Head Doll

Maker unidentified, but probably S.F.B.J.
French, c. 1907
18"

Bisque head, composition body and limbs; open mouth with row of upper teeth, paperweight eyes, human hair wig, pierced ears; swivel neck, fully jointed. Incised on back of head: "8". **(C)**

11-7 Dainty Dorothy
Sears, Roebuck & Co.
Chicago, Illinois, 1910
19½"

J.D. Kestner bisque shoulder head, kid body with bisque arms and lower legs; open mouth with four upper teeth, glass sleeping eyes with lashes, human hair wig; jointed at shoulders, hips, and knees. Oval label on chest: "Dainty Dorothy [outline of little girl]// Copyright 1910 by SEARS, ROEBUCK AND CO.//GERMANY". **(D)**

11-8 Wide-Awake Doll (left)
Butler Bros.
Sonneburg, Thür., 1914
8"

All-bisque doll; open-closed mouth with two upper teeth; painted eyes glancing to the side; painted shoes and socks; jointed at shoulders. Incised on back of body: "THE//"WIDE-AWAKE"//DOLL//REGISTERED//GERMANY//20". [This doll was very likely produced in competition with Kewpie dolls and came in three sizes: 4¾", 6¼", and 8".] **(E)**

Our Fairy (center)
Louis Wolf & Co.
Sonneberg, Thür., 1914
9"

All-bisque character doll; open-closed mouth with painted teeth,

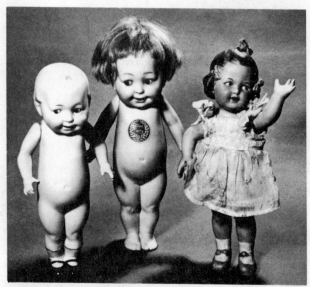

glass eyes glancing to the side, human hair wig; jointed at shoulders. Sticker on body: "Our Fairy//Germany". **(E)**

All-Bisque Girl (right)
Maker unidentified
Probably Germany, early 20th century
8"

All-bisque doll; open-closed mouth with row of teeth, intaglio eyes, molded and painted hair with lavender enameled ribbon across the back and bows at top and both sides, molded yellow shoes and white socks; jointed at shoulders. Body incised: "10490//3". **(D)**

11-9 Bisque-Head Boy (left)
Armand Marseille
Köppelsdorf, Thür., early 20th century
7½"

Bisque head, composition body and limbs; closed mouth, glass sleeping eyes glancing to the side ("goo-goo eyes"), human hair wig; swivel neck, jointed at shoulders and hips. Incised on back of head: "Germany//A 10/0 M". **(C)**

Bisque-Head Girl (right)
Ernst Heubach
Köppelsdorf, Thür., early 20th century
9"

Bisque head, composition body and limbs; closed mouth, glass eyes glancing to the side, human hair wig; swivel neck, jointed at shoulders

and hips. Incised on back of head: "Heubach. Köppelsdorf//322.1710 //Germany". **(D)**

11-10 Painted Bisque Doll

Ernst Heubach
Köppelsdorf, Thür., c. 1920-25
18"

Bisque head, composition body and limbs; open mouth, glass sleeping eyes with lashes, replacement wig; swivel neck, fully jointed. Incised on back of head: "Heubach—Köppelsdorf//Germany//251.4/0". [A good example of a bisque doll painted after the first firing and then lacquered without a second firing. Age has chipped the paint in many of these dolls.] **(E)**

12 | Parian (Untinted Bisque) Dolls

A type of porcelain resembling marble and extensively used for figure-modeling, **authentic** Parian was an English innovation that spread to the Continent and became immensely popular in the doll-manufacturing areas of Thuringia, where its soft, ivory tone and silken appearance were soon imitated in making fashionable dolls for the wealthy. The term "Parian" applied to dolls is nothing more than highly polished, basically untinted bisque. Nonetheless, Parian dolls are among the most exquisite bisque dolls made because they were intended to be **objets d'art** for fashion-conscious adults. To this end, German doll makers took pride in creating unusual hair styles, ornate headdresses, and decorations such as flowers, combs, and bows. Parian dolls originally sold for high prices since great care had to be taken in their manufacture: Any errors, cracks, or imperfections in white bisque dolls could not be covered over with glaze or color.

12-O Parian Lady with Blonde Hair (color plate, left)
Maker unknown
German, c. 1850-60
21" (entire doll), 5½" (shoulder head)

Untinted bisque shoulder head on cloth body with kid forearms; closed mouth, molded and painted features and hair; jointed at shoulders, hips, and knees. **(C)**

Parian Boy with Blonde Hair (color plate, right)
Maker unidentified
German, c. 1850-60
20" (entire doll), 5" (shoulder head)

Untinted bisque shoulder head on kid body with bisque forearms and cloth lower legs; closed mouth, molded and painted features and hair; jointed at shoulders, elbows, hips, and knees. **(C)**

12-1 Parian Doll with Brown Hair
Maker unidentified
German, c. 1850
4½" (shoulder head alone)

Untinted bisque shoulder head with molded and painted features and rare brown hair on body of later period. [Correct body should be muslin with arms of either parian or brown kid and parian feet.] **(D)**

12-2 Parian Doll
Maker unidentified
German, mid-19th century
23" (entire doll), 7" (shoulder head)

Untinted bisque shoulder head, cloth body and legs, kid arms; molded and painted features, molded and painted blonde hair, molded collar, bodice, and buttons on breast plate; jointed at shoulders, hips, and knees; original clothing. **(C)**

12-3 Parian Doll
Maker unidentified
German, mid-19th century
24" (entire doll)
7" (shoulder head)

Untinted bisque shoulder head on cloth body with brown kid arms and legs; molded and painted features and blonde hair; original clothing, including shoes. [A very fine example of a parian doll.] **(C)**

12-4 Parian Doll
Maker unidentified
German, mid-19th century
20" (entire doll)
5½" (shoulder head)

Untinted bisque shoulder head, cloth body and legs, kid arms; molded and painted features, molded and painted blonde hair, molded collar, bodice, and ribbon (collar and ribbon glazed) on breast plate, molded and glazed green lace head-covering at back of head; jointed at shoulders and hips. **(C)**

12-5 Parian Doll
Maker unknown
German, 19th century
23" (entire doll)
5" (shoulder head)

Untinted bisque shoulder head on cloth body with brown kid arms and legs; molded and painted features and blonde hair; molded collar with glazed pink bands. **(D)**

12-6 George and Martha Washington
Designed by Martha O. Ayers
Emma C. Clear
Los Angeles, California, 1947
19½" (Martha), 21½" (George)

Untinted bisque head on cloth body with untinted bisque lower limbs; molded and painted features; jointed at shoulders, hips, and knees. Incised on back of breast plates: "47 Clear [in script]". **(Each, D)**

13 | Metal Head Dolls

Although silver dolls had been made for royalty since the Middle Ages, dolls' heads of more common metals became prominent only in the last quarter of the 19th century, lasting in popularity (primarily in the United States) until the use of composition became widespread by 1930. Metal dolls' heads were made of pewter (now rare collector's items), brass, zinc, copper, and sheet metal, but today's collector is most likely to find examples in tin or aluminum, with most of these made in Germany.

Metal heads were made by René Poulin and Lucien Vervelle in France, Joseph Schön in Germany, and The Art Metal Works, Atlas Doll & Toy Co., Amor Metal Toy Stamping Co., and Giebeler-Falk in the United States. The best known metal-headed dolls, however, are Alfred Heller's "Diana," Karl Standfuss's "Juno," and, most popular of all, Buschow & Beck's "Minerva," also made by A. Vischer & Co. Minerva heads were usually made of brass and, after 1907, a "new process combination celluloid washable enamel," designed to overcome the chief drawback of metal heads: chipping and flaking.

13-O Minerva Metal-Head Doll (color plate)
Buschow & Beck
Reichenbach, Silesia, c. 1894-1915
19" (entire doll), 5½" (shoulder head)

Metal shoulder head, cloth body with composition forearms; open mouth with four upper teeth, glass eyes, molded and painted hair; jointed at shoulders and hips. Embossed on front of breast plate: "MINERVA/[Greek warrior's helmet]". Embossed on rear of breast plate: "6¼". [Doll is photographed together with identical Minerva shoulder head, but in a different size—6½"—marked at rear, "8".] **(Doll, D; head, E)**

13-1 Minerva Metal-Head Doll
Buschow & Beck
Reichenbach, Silesia, after 1894
13" (entire doll)
3" (shoulder head)

Metal shoulder head on cloth body with kid arms and legs; molded and painted features and hair, glass eyes; jointed at shoulders, hips, and knees. Embossed on front of breast plate: "MINERVA" [over Roman warrior's helmet]; embossed on back of shoulder plate: "GERMANY 9". **(E)**

**13-2 Minerva Metal-Head Doll
Buschow & Beck
Reichenbach, Silesia, c. 1900
19½" (entire doll)
5" (shoulder head)**

Metal shoulder head, cloth body and limbs; molded and painted features and hair; jointed at shoulders and hips. Embossed on front of breast plate: "PATENT". Embossed on rear of breast plate: "6". [A 1900 advertisement shows a Minerva head marked, "PATENT".] **(D)**

**13-3 Metal-Head Baby
Maker and place unidentified
Early 20th century
20"**

Enameled metal shoulder head on cloth body with metal arms and composition lower legs; open mouth with two upper teeth and tongue, metal sleeping eyes, painted and molded hair; jointed at shoulders and hips; voice box. **(E)**

**13-5 Aluminum-Head Doll
Giebeler-Falk Doll Corp.
New York City, 1919
25"**

**13-4 Metal-Head Doll
Maker unidentified
German, early 20th century
20" (entire doll)
4½" (shoulder head)**

Metal shoulder head on kid body with composition forearms; molded and painted features and hair; jointed at shoulders, hips, and knees. Paper label on chest; [sunflower within flowing ribbon; on ribbon:] "METAL HEAD//UNBREAK-ABLE." At left of label: "GERMANY". **(E)**

Aluminum head, wooden body and limbs with aluminum hands and feet; open-closed mouth with four painted upper teeth, brown metal sleeping eyes, originally with human hair wig; swivel neck, fully jointed (including ankles). Incised on back of head: "25//G [within six-pointed star]//U.S. PAT." Ribbon label (originally on dress): "Gie-Fa [in Gothic letters]//Trade Mark//New York, N.Y.//Aluminum Heads & Hands//Guaranteed Unbreakable". **(D)**

13-6 Aluminum-Head Doll
New England Doll Co.
Holyoke, Massachusetts, 1921
24"

Aluminum head on papier-mâché body with wooden arms and legs, aluminum hands, open-closed mouth with four painted teeth, brown metal sleeping eyes, human hair wig; swivel neck, fully jointed. Stamped on back of body: "NEDCO//DOLL". **(E)**

13-7 Metal Ball-Jointed Doll
A. Bucherer
Amriswil, Switzerland, 1921
7½"

Composition head, hands, and shoes on metal body; painted and molded features; fully jointed (including ankles). Incised on body: "MADE IN//SWITZERLAND//PATENTS//APPLIED FOR". [A series of these dolls appeared as policemen, firemen, clowns, comic-strip characters, etc. The metal joints come apart and are brought together by suction.] **(E)**

14 | Celluloid Dolls

Celluloid, a mixture of camphor and cellulose nitrate, was the first man-made plastic material used in manufacturing dolls. Although the practical use of celluloid had been demonstrated in 1869 when John Wesley Hyatt responded to the prize of $100,000 offered by a billiard ball company to anyone discovering a material which could be substituted for ivory, the first patent for a celluloid doll was granted M.C. Lefferts & W.B. Carpenter (later the Celluloid Manufacturing Co. of New York City) in 1881. The word "celluloid" is a trade name derived from cellulose contained in raw cotton, which, treated to a weak solution of nitric acid, is transformed into a substance very much like paper pulp. After being cleansed of the acid, the pulp is partially dried, mixed with camphor gum, rolled into sheets, and dried on hot cylinders. When softened by steam, celluloid is easily worked in molds.

Like any new substance, celluloid was originally expensive, but as it came to be produced in abundance—especially for dolls' heads, faces, bodies, and hands—its price dropped, together with its popularity. The best-known celluloid dolls of reasonable quality are those carrying the turtle mark of the Rheinische Gummi und Celluloid Fabrik; this firm's quality heads for Kämmer & Reinhardt, made in molds originally used for bisque dolls, are collector's prizes today. The chief disadvantages of celluloid are its extreme glossiness, its tendency to fade in sunlight, and its unfortunate ability to be squashed by exuberant children.

14-O Black and White Celluloid Babies (color plate)
Société National Française
Paris, 20th century
23"

Celluloid heads on celluloid bent-limb baby bodies; closed mouths, celluloid eyes (sleeping eyes on white baby), molded and painted hair; swivel necks, jointed at shoulders and hips. Incised on back of head and on body: "France//SNF [within diamond]". **(Each, E)**

14-1 Celluloid Doll
**Rheinische Gummi und Celluloid
   Fabrik Co.**
**Mannheim-Neckarau, Bavaria,
   early 20th century**
11½" (entire doll)
3½" (shoulder head)

Celluloid shoulder head on cloth body with celluloid hands; molded and painted features and hair; jointed at shoulders, hips, and knees. Embossed on back of shoulder plate: "GERMANY// [turtle mark]//SCHUTZ MARKE//8½". **(F)**

14-2 Celluloid Doll
Maker and place unidentified
Early 20th century
24" (entire doll)
6" (shoulder head)

Celluloid shoulder head on kid body with celluloid forearms and legs; open mouth with four upper teeth, brown glass sleeping eyes, human hair wig; jointed at shoulders, elbows, hips, and knees. **(E)**

14-3 Miniature Celluloid Doll
Rheinische Gummi and
**   Celluloid Fabrik Co.**
Mannheim-Neckarau, Bavaria,
**   after 1902**
5"

All-celluloid doll with molded shoes and stockings; molded and painted features and hair; jointed at shoulders and hips; original clothing. Embossed on body: "GERMANY//[turtle mark]//SCHUTZ MARKE". **(F)**

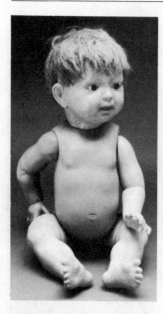

**14-4 Celluloid Character Baby
J.D. Kestner, Jr.
Waltershausen, Thür., c. 1914
10"**

Celluloid head on celluloid bent-limb baby body; open-closed mouth, glass eyes, human hair wig; swivel neck, jointed at shoulders and hips. Embossed on back of head: "Made in Germany//J.D.K. [illegible] 60". Embossed on back of body: "J.D.K.//203/7//GERMANY". **(E)**

15 | Composition Dolls

Perhaps no term is used more inconsistently by doll collectors than "composition." Strictly speaking, composition is any substance made of various ingredients mixed together. If this definition were taken literally, then composition dolls would include those made of papier-mâché, celluloid, vinyl, and many other materials. When a modern collector speaks of a composition doll, however, the plaything generally has a head made of a glue process or a wood pulp mixture. These, collectively, are the "compos" that were made in the 20th century, their popularity accelerated during World War I when German bisques were unavailable, and their infinite variety demonstrated in the '30s and '40s, before the age of vinyl.

It is no mere simplification to suggest that the primacy of composition in the United States after 1930 virtually ended American dependence on German imports and witnessed the flowering of such American-based manufacturers as Ideal, Horsman, Alexander, and EFFanBEE. The dolls in this section can only hint at the abundance of composition dolls produced, and additional "compos" are illustrated in the chapters on EFFanBEE (48) and Madame Alexander (49),

as well as those on portrait dolls (23), cartoon character dolls (24),
Kewpies (28), and Campbell Kids (29).

15-O Marilee Mama Doll (color plate)
EFFanBEE
New York City, c. 1925-30
30"

Composition shoulder head, cloth body with composition arms and
legs; open mouth with four upper teeth, metal sleeping eyes with
lashes, human hair wig; jointed at shoulders and hips; voice box. Embossed on back of breast plate: "[within oval] EFFANBEE//MARILEE//
COPR.//DOLL". **(E)**

**15-2 Early Composition
   Shoulder-Head Doll
Maker unidentified
German, early 20th century
12" (entire doll)
3" (shoulder head)**

Composition shoulder head on
cloth body with kid forearms and
feet; molded and painted features and molded blonde hair,
glass eyes; finish on shoulder
head almost bisque-like; jointed
at shoulders, hips, and knees.
[Very similar to the "Superior" dolls
made at this time; mark, however,
is obliterated.] **(E)**

**15-1 Early Composition
   Shoulder-Head Doll
Maker and place unidentified
c. 1890-1900
17"**

Composition shoulder head on
cloth body with composition
hands; molded and painted features and hair; jointed at shoulders and hips; original clothing.
Unmarked. **(E)**

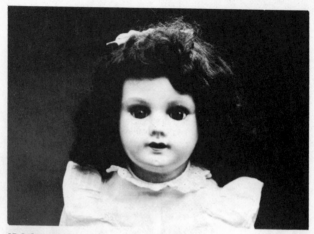

15-3 Composition Doll
Maker unidentified
Probably French, c. 1922
19"

Composition head, limbs, and body; open mouth with upper teeth, glass sleeping eyes with lashes, human hair wig; swivel neck, fully jointed. Incised on back of head and at base of neck (front): "8". [Doll was possibly made by Unis France.]

15-4 Composition Shoulder-Head Doll

Possibly New Doll Co.
New York City, 1923
21"

Composition shoulder head on cloth body with composition forearms
and lower legs; open mouth, metal sleeping eyes, human hair wig;
jointed at shoulders and hips. Embossed on back of shoulder plate:
"N.D. Co.// ©1923." **(F)**

15-5 Composition Babies
E.I. Horsman & Aetna Doll Co.
New York City, c. 1925
14" (each)

Composition heads on cloth bodies, with composition bent limbs;
open mouths, metal sleeping eyes, molded and painted hair; flange
necks, jointed at shoulders and hips; voice boxes. Embossed on back
of heads: "E.I.H. CO." **(F)**

15-6 Composition-Head Boy
Maker unidentified
American, c. 1930
25"

Composition head on cloth body with composition arms and legs; open mouth with four plastic teeth, brown metal sleeping eyes with lashes, molded and painted hair; flange neck, jointed at shoulders and hips. **(F)**

15-7 Nannette
Arranbee Doll Co.
New York City, c. 1934
25"

Composition shoulder head on cloth body with composition arms and legs; open mouth with three upper teeth, metal eyes with brown glass pupils; jointed at shoulders and hips. Unmarked. [Photographed without slouch hat that completes original costume.] **(E)**

II GENERIC TYPES

16 | Fashion Dolls

The use of dolls to show the current fashions in European capitals dates back to at least the 12th century and continued until the time of Napoleon I. Although the practice was of particular importance before the flowering of fashion magazines in the mid-19th century, it was occasionally revived toward the end of the century, using dolls made by Jumeau, Calots, Roch, and other French manufacturers. (Jumeau, for example, advertised in 1897 that it dressed expensive dolls to be sent abroad "as fashion models.") Most of these dolls were lady dolls, but bébés were also employed to display the latest children's fashions.

The collector cannot always be certain whether or not an elegantly-dressed doll was intended to be a fashion mannequin since wealthy doll owners often vied with one another in dressing their dolls expensively and in the latest vogue for mere show. In this regard it would be well to observe the shrewd comment of **The Collector's Encyclopedia of Dolls:** "Actually, a 'Fashion Doll' is not a type of doll but rather a functional use of dolls. Nearly any type of doll could be dressed in the latest adult or children's fashions and be sent out to show current styles."

16-0 French Fashion Doll (color plate left)
Maison Jumeau
Paris, c. 1865
14"

Bisque shoulder head, kid body and limbs; closed mouth, paperweight eyes, human hair wig, pierced ears; swivel neck. Incised on back of head: "2". Original clothing. **(B)**

French Fashion Doll (color plate right)
Maison Jumeau
Paris, 19th century
14"

Bisque shoulder head, kid body and limbs; closed mouth, paperweight eyes, human hair wig, pierced ears; swivel neck. Incised on back of head: "4". Original clothing. **(B)**

16-1 Milliner's Model
Maker unidentified
Probably French, c. 1830
8"

Papier-mâché head on unjointed kid body with carved wooden limbs; original clothing. [Style of dress suggests that doll was made in the 1830s.] **(C)**

**16-2 French Fashion Doll
Maison Jumeau
Paris, after 1878
15"**

Bisque socket head on bisque shoulder plate, cloth body with bisque limbs; closed mouth, glass eyes, pierced ears, human hair wig; swivel neck, jointed at shoulders and hips; original clothing. Stamped on body: "JUMEAU// MEDAILLE D'OR//PARIS". **(B)**

**16-3 French Fashion Doll
Probably F. Gaultier
Paris, late 19th century
10" (entire doll)
2½" (shoulder head)**

Bisque shoulder head on kid body; closed mouth, glass eyes, pierced ears, replacement wig; jointed at shoulders and hips. Incised on back of shoulder plate: "F G" (within shield). (Doll has been redressed.) **(C)**

17 | Baby Dolls

It comes as a surprise to many collectors that the sentimental and affectionate regard for babies that is almost universal today is a comparatively recent development in history (See Anita Schorsch's **Images of Childhood** for an engaging introduction to the history of childhood). Until the late 18th and early 19th centuries, there was very little differentiation made between a baby and a child, both being seen merely as miniature adults. And this is exactly the way babies were reflected in the world of dolls: They were portrayed as little adults, albeit a bit chubbier and with shorter limbs and necks than those of other dolls.

The first attempt to create a baby body that was completely unlike other dolls' bodies was probably Charles Motschmann's in 1857 (see 21-1), and this adaptation of oriental baby dolls was soon followed by the chubby Frozen Charlotte, undoubtedly meant to portray babies. The greatest innovation in the making of baby dolls, however, was the introduction in 1909 of Kämmer & Reinhardt's composition bent-limb baby bodies, known also as "Next to Nature" jointed bodies. This development, coupled with the almost simultaneous introduction of character faces, led to the production of more and more realistic-appearing baby dolls. The search for a baby doll that looked like a newborn babe (17-2) culminated in the worldwide fad for Bye-Lo Babies in the 1920s (see section 18) and a host of competing models on both sides of the Atlantic.

17-O Character Baby (color plate, left)
William Goebel
Oeslau, Thür., after 1909
21"

Bisque head on composition bent-limb baby body; open mouth with two upper teeth, brown glass sleeping eyes with lashes, human hair wig; swivel neck, jointed at shoulders and hips. Incised on back of head: "[crown]//WG [intertwined]//B5—//Germany". **(C)**

Character Baby #116A (color plate, right)
Kämmer & Reinhardt
Waltershausen, Thür., after 1909
19"

Simon & Halbig bisque head on composition bent-limb baby body; open-closed mouth with two painted upper teeth, glass sleeping eyes, human hair wig; swivel neck, jointed at shoulders and hips. Incised on back of head: "K [ampersand within six-pointed star] R//SIMON & HALBIG//116A". **(C)**

17-1 New Born Babe
Designed by Jeno Juszko
Louis Amberg & Son
New York City, 1914
12"

Bisque head on cloth body with composition hands; closed mouth, glass eyes, painted hair; flange neck, jointed at shoulders and hips. Incised on back of head: "©L.A.&S. 1914//#G 45520". [Apparently, the first doll to be modeled from a new-born infant. Reissued in the early 1920s during the height of the Bye-Lo Baby craze.] **(D)**

17-2 Lori
Probably S & Co.
Germany, after 1909
17½"

Bisque head on composition bent-limb baby body; open mouth with two lower teeth, brown glass eyes, molded and painted hair; swivel neck, jointed at shoulders and hips. Incised on back of head: "D// LORI//232//11". **(C)**

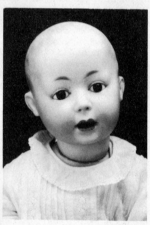

17-3 Century Doll
Century Doll Co.
New York City, after 1909
17"

Bisque head on cloth body with composition hands; closed mouth, glass eyes, molded and painted hair; jointed at shoulders and hips. Incised on back of head: "CENTURY DOLL Cº.//Kestner Germany". [These dolls were made by J.D. Kestner, Jr. for the Century Doll Co.] **(D)**

17-4 Georgene Averill Character Baby
German, early 20th century
16"

Bisque head on cloth body with composition hands and composition bent-limb legs; open mouth with two lower teeth and tongue, glass eyes, molded and painted hair; flange neck, jointed at shoulders and hips. Incised on back of head: "[in script] Copr. by// Georgene Averill/1905/3692/0// Germany". **(C)**

17-5 All-Biskoline Baby
Parsons-Jackson Co.
Cleveland, Ohio, c. 1915
10½"

Biskoline head on Biskoline bent-limb baby body; open mouth, molded and painted eyes and hair; steel spring joints at neck, shoulders, and hips. Embossed on back of head: "[outline of stork]// A6". Embossed on back of body: "[outline of stork]//TRADEMARK". [Biskoline was a substance, used by the Parsons-Jackson Co., that resembled celluloid.] **(D)**

17-6 Jutta-Baby
Cuno & Otto Dressel
Sonneberg, Thür., probably 1922
16"

Bisque head on composition bent-limb baby body; open mouth with tongue, glass sleeping eyes, human hair wig; swivel neck, jointed at shoulders, wrists, hips. Incised on back of head: "Jutta-Baby//Dressel//Germany//1922//11½". [Jutta was produced from 1908 through the 1920s.] **(C)**

17-7 My Dream Baby
Arranbee Doll Co.
New York City, c. 1924
15"

Armand Marseille bisque head on cloth body with celluloid hands; closed mouth, glass sleeping eyes, molded and painted hair; flange neck, jointed at shoulders, hips, and wrists; voice box. Incised on back of head: "A M//Germany//341.14". [Armand Marseille made the heads for My Dream Baby. The doll was designed to be competition for the Bye-Lo Baby. See also 17-8 and 33-3.] **(E)**

17-8 Open-Mouthed My Dream Baby
Armand Marseille
Köppelsdorf, Thür., c. 1924
15"

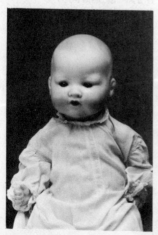

Bisque head on composition bent-limb baby body; open mouth with two lower teeth, glass eyes, molded and painted hair; swivel neck, jointed at shoulders and hips. Incised on back of head: "A M//Germany//351.14.K". [Called by collectors "Rock-a-bye Baby," although no evidence exists that doll was marketed under this name.] **(E)**

**17-9 Kiddiejoy
Jacobs & Kassler
New York City, 1925
14"**

Bisque head on cloth body with celluloid hands; closed mouth, glass sleeping eyes, molded and painted hair; flange neck, jointed at hips and wrists; voice box. Incised on back of head: "Germany //Kiddiejoy". On button: "JK//Kiddiejoy//New York". [Hitz, Jacobs & Kassler began to sell the Kiddiejoy doll in 1922; in 1925 the firm became Jacobs & Kassler. Armand Marseille made many of the Kiddiejoy heads. Kiddiejoy was a prime competitor of the Bye-Lo Baby.]

18 | Bye-Lo Babies

Grace Storey Putnam was a watercolorist who sacrificed her own early career in favor of her husband, who was a sculptor. After their divorce, it was necessary for her to seek a living and she became an art teacher. In the early 1920s she determined to create a doll in imitation of a baby about three days old and searched the hospitals of Los Angeles in search of a perfect model, finding one eventually in a Salvation Army home. After perfecting her wax model, she showed it to one of the officials at George Borgfeldt & Co. who was immediately taken with its commercial possibilities. Although Mrs. Putnam had originally wanted the doll made in rubber, Borgfeldt produced it in 1922 with a bisque socket head on a composition body (18-1). The Bye-Lo Baby was an instant success and became known, because of its enormous sales, as the "Million Dollar Baby." Within a year, it was produced with a bisque flange neck on a cloth body designed by Mrs. Putnam herself. The bisque heads were made by a number of German manufacturers, including Kestner, Kling, and Alt, Beck and Gottschalck, among others. Bye-Lo heads were made of composition as early as 1924 by the Cameo Doll Co. (18-2); of celluloid in 1925 by Karl Standfuss; of wood in 1925 by Schoenhut (47-8); and all-bisque Bye-Los were manufactured by Kestner beginning in 1925 (18-5). The Bye-Lo craze of the 1920s set off fierce competition among doll manufacturers for realistic baby dolls, and several of these competing dolls are illustrated in the preceding section.

18-0 Bye-Lo Baby (color plate)
Designed by Grace Storey Putnam
German, c. 1924
13"

Bisque head on cloth bent-limb ("frog") baby body with celluloid hands; closed mouth, brown sleeping eyes, molded and painted hair; flange neck, jointed at shoulders and wrists; voice box. Incised on back of head: "Copr. by [in script] //Grace S. Putnam [in script] //MADE IN GERMANY". **(D)**

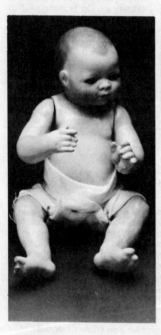

18-1 Early Bye-Lo Baby
Designed by Grace Storey Putnam
German, 1923
12"

Bisque head on composition bent-limb baby body; closed mouth, sleeping eyes, molded and painted hair; swivel neck, jointed at shoulders and hips. Incised on back of head: "© 1923 by//Grace S. Putnam//MADE IN GERMANY// 1369/30. [The first Bye-Lo Babies had bisque socket heads that fit on composition bodies. The eyes were also larger than those made after 1923. Celluloid hands were also added after 1923.] **(D)**

18-2 Bye-Lo Baby
Designed by Grace Storey Putnam
German, c. 1924
18"

Bisque head on cloth bent-limb ("frog") baby body with celluloid hands; closed mouth, brown sleeping eyes, molded and painted hair; flange neck, jointed at shoulders and wrists; voice box. Incised on back of head: "[in script] Copr. by//Grace S. Putnam [in script]//MADE IN GERMANY". **(D)**

18-3 Bye-Lo Baby
Designed by Grace Storey
  Putnam
German, c. 1924
14"

Same as 18-2, except that sleeping eyes are blue; original clothing. **(D)**

18-4 Bye-Lo Baby
Designed by Grace Storey
  Putnam
Germany, c. 1924
12"

Same as 18-2. **(D)**

18-5 All-Bisque Bye-Lo Babies
J.G. Kestner, Jr.
Waltershausen, Thür., 1925

5" (each)

All-bisque dolls, jointed at shoulders and hips; painted features. Incised on back of body: "20-12//Copr. by//Grace S. Putnam//Germany [all in script]". **(Each E)**

18-6 Laughing Bye-Lo Baby Designed by Grace Storey Putnam
German, c. 1925
20"

Bisque head on cloth bent-limb baby body; open-closed mouth, glass eyes, molded and painted hair; flange neck, jointed at shoulders and hips. Incised on back of head: "Copr. by//Grace S. Putnam//Germany." Button on body: "HYGIENIC A1 TOYS//DEAN'S RAG// BOOK C° L^{td}//MADE IN ENGLAND". **(B)**

18-7 Composition Bye-Lo Baby Designed by Grace Storey Putnam
Cameo Doll Co.
New York City, 1924-25
12"

Composition head on cloth bent-limb baby body with composition hands; sleeping eyes, molded and painted features and hair; jointed at shoulders and hips. Embossed on back of head: "GRACE STOREY//PUTNAM". **(E)**

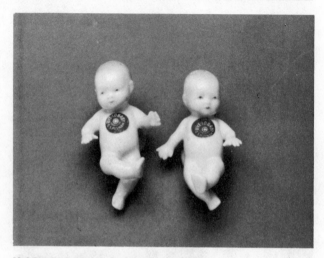

18-8 Bye-Lo Baby Salt and Pepper Shakers
Designed by Grace Storey Putnam
German, late 1920s
3" long (each)

China dolls with casters in head, corked hole for filling at base. Label on chest: "BYE-LO BABY//© GERMANY//G.S. PUTNAM". **(Pair, C)**

19 | Lady Dolls

Before the 19th century ladies and children dressed almost identically, and most manufactured dolls, consequently, served as ladies or as children, depending on how their owners wished to dress them. By the 1860s and '70s, however, the then-new bisque heads were popularized around the world by elegant French lady dolls, dressed in the height of fashion, and known as "Parisiennes." The vogue for dressing lady dolls in the latest fashions continued well into the 20th century (and, of course, continues today), and clothing could be purchased ready-made at such fine shops as A la Poupée de Nurenberg, Au Nain Bleu, and Madame Barrois, or they could be sewn and fashioned at home by the child herself as a lesson in dressmaking that would hold her in good stead as an adult. (A ladies' magazine of 1901 warned that no self-respecting mother should allow her daughter to be seen in public with a doll wearing last season's clothes.)

There is some confusion among experts about the term "lady doll." Some, like Constance King, believe that fashion dolls (see section 16) never existed at all and call all dolls dressed in the latest adult vogue "lady dolls" or "Parisiennes." Others, like the Colemans, present hard evidence that fashion dolls did in fact exist and indicate that lady dolls were occasionally used, long after the advent of fashion magazines, to demonstrate the newest styles abroad. The Colemans illustrate as well that not all lady dolls were French-made.

19-0 Gibson Girl (color plate)
J.D. Kestner, Jr.
Waltershausen, Thür., c. 1910
20½" (entire doll), 7½" (shoulder head)

Bisque shoulder head, kid body and limbs with bisque forearms; closed mouth, brown glass sleeping eyes with lashes, human hair wig; jointed at shoulders, elbows, hips, and knees; original clothing. Stamped in blue on chest: "Gibson Girl". Label on chest: "[crown with two ribbons] JDK Germany//½ cork stuffed". **(B)**

19-1 Lady Doll
Maison Huret
Paris, c. 1880
16"

Bisque shoulder head, cloth body with bisque arms and cloth legs; closed mouth, paperweight eyes, pierced ears; swivel neck, jointed at shoulders and hips. Stamped on body: "HURET". **(B)**

19-2 La Georgienne
A. Lanternier & Cie.
Limoges, France, c. 1900
17"

Bisque head, composition body and limbs; open-closed mouth with row of upper teeth, brown glass eyes, pierced ears, human hair wig; fully jointed. Incised on back of head: "FABRICATION//FRANÇAISE [within box]//FAVORITE//No. 3//Ed Tasson [in script]//A L & C^(ie)//LIMOGES". Stamped below mark: "DÉPOSÉ// [woman's head with flowing tresses]// LA GEORGIENNE". **(C)**

19-3 Gibson-type Lady Doll
Heinrich Handwerck
Gotha, Thür., c. 1910
23"

Bisque head, composition body and limbs; closed mouth, intaglio eyes, pierced ears, human hair wig; swivel neck, fully jointed. Incised on back of head: "10". Stamped on left thigh: "Handwerck//Germany". [In 1910 Borgfeldt announced that it was distributing a line of Handwerck character dolls with women's faces.] **(D)**

19-4 Character Lady Doll
Maker and place unknown
Probably early 20th century
13"

Bisque head, composition body and limbs; open mouth with three upper teeth, brown glass eyes, human hair wig; swivel neck, fully jointed. Incised on back of head; "MI". **(C)**

19-5 Bisque Shoulder Head
Maker and place unidentified
Late 19th century
27" (entire doll)
5½" (shoulder head)

Bisque shoulder head, cloth body and legs, kid arms; turned head, closed mouth, glass sleeping eyes, and human hair wig; jointed at shoulders, hips, and knees. Unmarked. [Notice high breast and fine modeling of head and shoulders.] **(C)**

19-6 Florodora (left)
Armand Marseille
Köppelsdorf, Thür., after 1909
16"

Bisque head, composition body and limbs; open mouth with four teeth, glass sleeping eyes, replacement wig; swivel neck, fully jointed. Incised on back of head: "Made in Germany [in script]//Florodora [in script]//A 2/0 + M". [The first Florodoras, registered in Germany in 1901 by George Borgfeldt, had kid bodies and Armand Marseille heads. After 1909, Marseille began to use bisque Florodora heads on composition bodies.] **(E)**

Bisque Shoulder Head Doll (right)
Maker unidentified
German, early 20th century
16" (entire doll), 5" (shoulder head)

Bisque shoulder head on kid body with bisque forearms; open mouth with four upper teeth, human hair wig; jointed at shoulders, hips, and knees. Incised on back of shoulder plate: "Made in Germany [in script]". [Doll is very likely an Armand Marseille.] **(E)**

19-7 Queen Louise (left)
Louis Wolf & Co.
New York City, c. 1910
21"

Armand Marseille bisque head, composition body and limbs; open mouth with four upper teeth, glass sleeping eyes with lashes, human hair wig; swivel neck, fully jointed. Incised on back of head: ''Germany//Queen Louise''. [Queen Louise heads were made by Armand Marseille for Louis Wolf & Co.] **(D)**

Queen Louise (right)
Louis Wolf & Co.
New York City, c. 1910
19"

Same as previous description, except for mark on back of head: "Queen Louise//Germany//5". **(D)**

20 | Mechanical Dolls

The great age of automata was the 18th century when the nobility of Europe delighted in the mechanical inventions of genius made for them by the great clockmakers of the Continent. Anyone who has visited the grottoes of 18th-century European palaces realizes how these ingenious mechanical displays can still completely disarm the most sophisticated traveler more than two centuries after their invention. The 19th century, however, witnessed a falling away of genius as mechanical toys and dolls were mass produced for the middle classes, but these products, ranging from dolls that perform simple movements upon music-box bases to those that walk and push perambulators, are by modern standards infinitely more satisfying and engaging than the unimaginative products of today. The mechanical dolls illustrated in this section can only suggest the great variety produced in the 19th and early 20th centuries; the mechanism of each is described in the entries that follow.

20-0 Walking Doll (color plate)
William Farr Goodwin, inventor
George H. Hawkins, maker of shoulder head

New York City, c. 1868
11" (doll)

Cloth-reinforced papier-mâché shoulder head on wooden torso with wooden hands and composition feet on jointed iron legs. Clockwork mechanism propels wheeled vehicle, causing doll to "walk." G.H. Hawkins' label on back of breast plate: "X.L.C.R. [phonetic equivalent of 'Excelsior']//DOLL HEAD//Pat. Sept. 8, 1868". **(B)**

20-1 Autoperipatetikos
Patented by Enoch Rice Morrison
Probably New York City, after 1862
10"

China shoulder head, kid arms; paper cone under skirt houses clockwork mechanism that activates metal boots; key wound. Printed on paper disk: "Patented July 15th, 1862; also, in Europe, 20th Dec. 1862. This Doll is only intended to walk on a smooth surface." **(C)**

20-2 Musical Knitting Doll
Maison Jumeau
Paris, 1873
18", including base

Bisque head connected by steel rods to papier-mâché body (housing mechanism) with steel-rod limbs and composition forearms and lower legs; open mouth with row of upper teeth, paperweight eyes, pierced ears, human hair wig. Incised on back of head: "TETE JUMEAU". [Key-wound mechanism operates music box and causes doll to move head

and "knit." Doll was awarded a gold medal at the Vienna Exposition of 1873.] **(B)**

20-3 Tea-Drinking Automaton
Maker unidentified
Limoges, France, 19th century
Doll: 14" (seated); base: 6"

Bisque head, composition hands, cloth legs; open mouth with four teeth, brown glass eyes, human hair wig; clothing conceals steel rods that move head and arms. [Operated by key wind and plunger that cause music to play and doll to "drink" tea from a miniature gold lustre ware tea set.] **(B)**

20-4 Clown with Performing Bears
Probably J. Caron
Paris, c. 1882
Clown (8"), bears (8"), base (4")

Bisque head, wire body with bisque forearms and legs; molded and painted features, glass eyes, human hair wig. Incised on back of head: "1/JC/S1". [Key at base activates clockwork mechanism; clown turns and bears perform acrobatic tricks.] **(B)**

20-5 Walking Doll
Roullet & Decamps
Paris, c. 1895
15"

Bisque head, composition body
and limbs; open mouth with row of
upper teeth, brown glass eyes,
pierced ears, human hair wig;
arms jointed at shoulders and
wrists, legs unjointed and connected by steel rods to clockwork
mechanism which, when wound,
causes doll to walk. Incised on
back of head: "4". Key marked: "R
D". [Head probably made by
Maison Jumeau.] **(C)**

20-6 Mechanical Doll
Maker unidentified
German, c. 1900
13½"

Bisque socket head connected
by a wooden stick to a wooden
back and a thin wood-covered
"bellows" trunk; wire upper arms
and legs with papier-mâché
forearms and legs; open mouth
with four upper teeth, glass eyes,
human hair wig. Incised on back
of head: "6". Label on bellows:
"D.R. [for Deutsches Reich] Patent
//No. 56996". [When stomach is
pressed, music box plays and doll
crashes cymbals.] **(D)**

20-7 Swimming Doll
Rheinische Gummi und Celluloid
    Fabrik Co.
Mannheim-Neckarau, Bavaria,
    early 20th century
16"

Celluloid shoulder head on cork
body with composition limbs;
open mouth with four upper teeth,
glass eyes, human hair wig;
jointed at shoulders, hips, knees.
Embossed on back of head: "[pic-
ture of turtle]//SCHUTZ MARKE".
[Key wind in stomach activates
clockwork mechanism between
two halves of body; limbs move in
swimming position. Doll floats and
"swims" in water.] **(D)**

20-8 Bell-ringing Mechanical Dolls

Simon & Halbig head (girl)
Th. Recknagel head (boy)
German, after 1905
Dolls (each 8"), lower base (3")

Both dolls: bisque head, cloth over steel rod body and limbs, composition forearms and lower legs; open mouth with upper teeth, glass eyes. Incised on back of girl's head: "SIMON & HALBIG//S & H//Germany". Incised on back of boy's head: "R 10/0 A" [for Th. Recknagel of Alexandrinenthal]. [Crank-operated mechanism operates music box and causes dolls to move heads and ring bells.] **(C)**

20-9 Musical-Mechanical Doll
Simon & Halbig (head)
Maker of mechanism
**   unidentified**
German or French, after 1905
15"

Simon & Halbig bisque head on papier-mâché cone (housing mechanism), with bisque forearms; cone rests on three wheels, with rear wheel activated by the mechanism; open mouth with four upper teeth, glass sleeping eyes with lashes, pierced ears, human hair wig. Incised on back of head: "SIMON & HALBIG//S & H//5½". [Winding key near base activates music box and clockwork mechanism, causing doll to move arms and "dance" to a Chopin waltz.] **(B)**

**20-10 Mechanical Baby Doll
Armand Marseille
Köppelsdorf, Thür., after 1909
24"**

Bisque head on composition bent-limb baby body; trap door in stomach reveals mechanism; open mouth with two upper teeth, glass eyes, mohair wig; socket head attached to mechanism, jointed at shoulders and hips. Incised on back of head: "G 327 B// D.R.G.M. 259//A 14 M". [Key wind in left side activates clockwork mechanism; doll's eyes open and close and head moves from side to side. Made for a distributor with the initials "G.B.," probably George Borgfeldt.] **(D)**

**20-11 Dolly Walker
Patented by Harry Coleman
Wood Toy Co.
New York City, 1917-23
28"**

Composition shoulder head, wooden frame body with wire mesh torso, wooden upper arms and legs, composition forearms; open mouth with two upper teeth, painted eyes, human hair wig. Stamped on bottom of torso: "Oct 6 1919". [Original advertisements claimed that this doll could "sit, kneel, dance, and sleep."] **(E)**

21 | Talking Dolls

There have been attempts to make dolls "talk" for centuries. "The principal methods," the Colemans write, "are by pulling strings, exerting pressure on some part of the body, moving one or more of the limbs of the doll, or by changing its position. Bellows were used to produce sound at an early date, and in the 19th century reeds were placed in dolls' bodies and sound produced by blowing across them. The most realistic types of talking dolls were those that contained a phonograph." Examples of most of these are found in the pages that follow.

21-O Dolly Reckord (color plate)
Averill Manufacturing Co.
New York City, 1922-23
25"

Composition shoulder head, cloth body with composition arms and lower legs; open mouth with two upper teeth and tongue, metal sleeping eyes, human hair wig; jointed at shoulders and hips; crank to wind phonograph at left side of body, sound box in front, phonograph at rear. Stamped on body: "A MADAME HENDREN//DOLL//228//MADE IN U.S.A." [Cylinder records include: "Now I Lay Me," "Rock-a-Bye-Baby," "Little Boy Blue," "One Two," and "London Bridge." Each record is stamped: "AVERILL MANUFACTURING CO//NEW YORK CITY U.S.A."] **(D)**

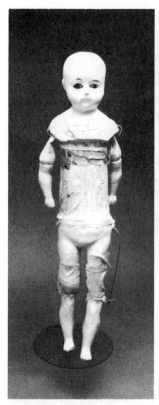

21-2 Lynd Speaking and Singing
Doll
Patented by William John Lynd
Yreka, California, 1886
14"

Bisque head, composition body
and limbs; open mouth, glass
eyes, molded eyebrows, human
hair wig; swivel neck, fully jointed
(except wrists). Incised on back of
head: "06". [A speaking tube inserted in the back of the head
could cause "sound from the human voice to appear to proceed
from the figure of a doll."] **(B)**

21-1 Talking Waxed Doll
(Motschmann Type)
Maker unidentified
Probably German, c. 1860
14"

Wax over papier-mâché shoulder
head, twill over papier-mâché torso, papier-mâché pelvic area,
wood and twill cloth limbs; glass
eyes; floating joints. [Pull-string
causes doll to squeak "Ma-Ma."]
(D)

21-3 Bébé Phonographe
Maison Jumeau
Paris, 1893-98
22"

Bisque head, composition body and limbs; open mouth with fourteen
upper teeth, paperweight eyes, pierced ears, human hair wig; swivel
neck, fully jointed. Incised on back of head: "DÉPOSÉ//TETE JUMEAU".
[A cylinder phonograph is contained within the chest and is operated
by a key wind and plunger in the back. Cylinders can be changed by
removing the metal chest plate, which is pierced to act as the speaker.
Cylinders are marked, "JUMEAU PHONOGRAPHE".] **(A)**

21-4 Talking Bébé Jumeau in
Original Box
Maison Jumeau/S.F.B.J.
Paris, 1900
24"

21-5 Pull-String Talking Doll
Probably S.F.B.J.
French, early 20th century
22"

Bisque head, composition body and limbs; open mouth with four upper teeth, glass sleeping eyes with lashes, molded eyebrows, pierced ears, human hair wig; swivel neck, fully jointed. Incised on back of head: "26". [Body cut open for insertion of voice box; two pull cords cause doll to say "Mama" and "Papa." Original clothing marked (in script): "Au Nain Bleu//406-a-412 Rue St. Honoré//Paris". Au Nain Bleu distributed S.F.B.J. dolls.] **(B)**

Bisque head, composition body and limbs; closed mouth, glass eyes, pierced ears, cork crown, human hair wig; swivel neck, fully jointed; body cut open to insert voice box; original clothing. On back of head: black check mark. Body unmarked. [Information on box identifies doll as No. 11 and is dated 1900. In 1899 the Jumeau name was being carried on by S.F.B.J.] **(B)**

22 | Character Doll

A kind of complacency characterized the doll industry in the closing years of the 19th century. Business had never been better, nor production higher, and the smiling dolly-faced bisques that virtually sold themselves in the shops began to look very much alike, no matter the maker. This complacency was shattered at a major exhibition of dolls in Munich in 1908. Here, a gathering of talented artists, including seamstresses, painters, sculptors, and woodcarvers, exhibited a new type of doll, a doll intended to be as true to life as possible. Although the "art doll" was not originally meant to be mass produced, the works exhibited in Munich had great repercussions in the Thuringian centers of manufacture. Kämmer & Reinhardt reacted first by commissioning a Berlin artist to design a doll that would resemble as closely as possible a six-week-old child. The result, "Baby" (see 39-2), was an immediate success and was followed by other realistic dolls. These "character dolls," so named by Franz Reinhardt, had rolls of fat, dimples, uneven features, and the sulky or even unhappy expressions of real babies. Although the public was at first slow to accept the succession of character dolls, and never abandoned the typical smiling-faced dolly, realistic dolls continued to be made and gradually embraced not only babies, but children of all ages and adults as well.

22-0 Character Boy (color plate)
Simon & Halbig
Gräferhain, Thür., after 1905
24"

Bisque head, composition body and limbs; closed mouth, painted eyes, mohair wig; swivel neck, fully jointed: redressed. Incised on back of head: "S & H//[illegible]/0". **(C)**

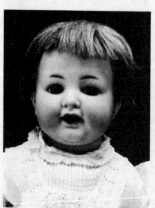

22-1 Character Baby
Kämmer & Reinhardt
Waltershausen, Thür., after 1909
21"

Simon & Halbig bisque head on composition bent-limb baby body; open mouth with two upper teeth and tongue, glass eyes, human hair wig; swivel neck, jointed at shoulders and hips. Incised on back of head: "K [ampersand within six-pointed star] R// SIMON & HALBIG// 126/50". **(D)**

22-2 Character Baby Boy
J.D. Kestner, Jr.
Waltershausen, Thür., after 1909
11"

Bisque head on composition bent-limb baby body; open mouth with two lower teeth, glass eyes, molded and painted hair; swivel neck, jointed at shoulders and hips. Incised on back of head: "J.D.K.// 7". **(E)**

22-3 Character Boy
Kley & Hahn
Ohrdruf, Thür., early 20th century
21"

Bisque head, composition body and limbs; closed mouth, intaglio eyes, human hair wig; swivel neck, fully jointed. Incised on back of head: "K & H [within banner]//520// 8½". **(C)**

22-4 Schoolboy
Maker unidentified
Probably German, early 20th century
19" (entire doll)
5½" (shoulder head)

Bisque turned shoulder head, cloth body with composition lower limbs; closed mouth, brown glass eyes, molded and painted blonde hair; jointed at shoulders and hips; wooden bellows in chest to produce sound. Incised on back of shoulder plate: "30/B 7½". [Head is turned to left.] **(E)**

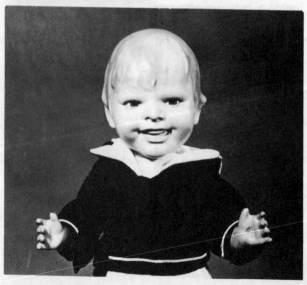

22-5 Gladdie
Designed by Helen W. Jensen
German, 1929-30
18½"

Composition head, cloth body with composition bent arms and lower legs; open mouth with undefined row of upper teeth, glass eyes, molded and painted hair; flange neck, jointed at shoulders and hips. Incised on back of head: [all in script] "Gladdie// Copyrighted By// Helen W. Jensen// Germany// 1005/1420/45". **(C)**

---

23 | Portrait Dolls

Famous people have always lent their features to dolls (Queen Victoria, for example, was commercially rendered in wax as early as 1840), but the large-scale manufacture of dolls representing celebrated personalities really began with the corresponding development of what we today call the mass media—particularly magazines, the movies, radio, and, most recently, television. That is, only when a figure could be known to virtually millions of people was it commercially feasible to peddle his likeness to an adoring public. for as charming as portrait dolls are, they actually represent the very most commercial aspect of doll production: Feeding off the momentary moment in the sun of a "personality," the doll manufacturer, particularly as the 20th century has advanced, has been quick to render three-dimensionally the two-dimensional heroes of the young.

Although wretched plastic likenesses of television and movie personalities flood the market today, the golden age of the portrait doll was the 1920's and '30's, when children's favorite movie stars, from Charlie Chaplin and Jackie Coogan to Deanna Durbin and Jane Withers were reproduced as dolls. Ideal's Shirley Temple doll, which sold more than a million and a half copies at the height of the Depression, is of course the subject of a book in itself and illustrates the profound influence that the mass media have had (and continue to have) in the selection of subject matter for modern dolls. Be that as it may, the acquisition of portrait dolls is among the most nostalgic and entertaining fields of contemporary doll collecting.

The portrait dolls illustrated in the following pages can only suggest the great variety available to collectors. Additional dolls appear in section 49 on Madame Alexander.

23-O Dionne Quintuplets (color plate)
Designed by Bernard Lipfert
Alexander Doll Co.
New York City, 1936
11" (each)

Composition heads and bent-limb baby bodies; closed mouths, brown metal sleeping eyes, human hair wigs; swivel necks, jointed at shoulders and hips. Embossed on back of bodies: "MADAME ALEXANDER". [Each doll wears a gold-colored metal name-pin: "Yvonne," "Annette," "Emelie," "Cecile," "Marie." Aside from these name-pins and variously colored outfits, the five dolls are otherwise identical.] **(Set, C)**

23-2 Fascist Doll in Likeness of Benito Mussolini
Maker and place unknown
c. 1925-30
19"

Composition head, body, and limbs; closed mouth, brown glass eyes; swivel neck, jointed at shoulders and hips; dressed in black shirt uniform of period; cap with Fascist emblem. **(C)**

23-1 John D. Rockefeller
Bernard Ravca
Paris, late 1920s
23"

Cloth doll with molded and painted stockinet face and cloth-over-wire body. **(D)**

23-3 Jane Withers (left)
Alexander Doll Co.
New York City, 1937
18"

All-composition doll; open mouth with six upper teeth, metal sleeping eyes with lashes, mohair wig; swivel neck, jointed at shoulders and hips; original clothing. Wears original gold-colored pin with name "Jane Withers" in script. Label on dress: "Jane Withers//ALL RIGHTS RESERVED//Madame Alexander, N.Y." **(D)**

Deanna Durbin (center)
Ideal Toy Corporation
New York City, 1939
21"

All-composition doll; open mouth with six upper teeth, metal eyes with lashes, human hair wig; swivel neck, jointed at shoulders and hips; Embossed on back of head: "IDEAL DOLL". [Unmarked copies of this doll were marketed as "Teenage Star," causing collectors of this day to believe that the doll was somehow meant to be passed on to the public as Judy Garland.] **(D)**

Shirley Temple (right)
Designed by Bernard Lipfert
Ideal Novelty & Toy Co.
New York City, c. 1935
18"

All-composition doll; open mouth with six upper teeth, hazel metal
sleeping eyes with lashes, mohair wig; swivel neck, jointed at shoulders
and hips; original clothing. Embossed on back of head: "18//SHIRLEY
TEMPLE//IDEAL//N & T Co." Label on dress: "Genuine [in script]//SHIRLEY
TEMPLE//DOLL//REGISTERED U.S. PAT. OFF.//IDEAL NOV. & TOY CO.//
MADE IN U.S.A." Original pin: "THE WORLD'S DARLING// [photograph
from the film **Bright Eyes**]//GENUINE SHIRLEY TEMPLE DOLL". **(D)**

23-4 Shirley Temple
Designed by Bernard Lipfert
Ideal Novelty & Toy Corporation
New York City, 1936
10½"

All-composition doll; open mouth
with six upper teeth, hazel metal
sleeping eyes with lashes, mohair
wig; swivel neck, jointed at shoulders and hips; original clothing.
Embossed on back of head: "SHIR-
LEY TEMPLE//COP. IDEAL//N & T
CO." Label on dress, and pin,
same as in previous entry. **(D)**

23-5 Fanny Brice as Baby Snooks
Ideal Novelty & Toy Co.
New York City, c. 1939
12"

Composition head and trunk with
flexible wire arms and legs, composition hands and feet. Embossed at back of head: "IDEAL
DOLL". Paper tag: "FLEXY//AN
IDEAL DOLL// Fanny Brice's [in

script]//BABY SNOOKS//IDEAL NOV-ELTY & TOY CO.//LONG ISLAND CI-TY, N.Y." On opposite side of tag: "The Doll//of //A Thousand//Poses// MADE IN U.S.A." **(E)**

23-6 Charlie McCarthy
Copyrighted by Charlie
McCarthy, Inc.
New York City, 1937
43"

Composition head on cloth body with composition forearms and boots; painted features, hinged lower jaw and mouth operated by pull cord from back of head. [Cloth legs unusually long to permit dummy to sit on lap à la Edgar Bergen.] **(D)**

24 | Cartoon Character and Storybook Dolls

Comic-strip and movie cartoon characters have been marketed as dolls from the earliest beginnings of tabloid journalism and the animated cimema. Such dolls as those made from Little Orphan Annie and Betty Boop are in every sense of the term "portrait dolls," since their personalities, known to millions of tabloid readers and moviegoers of the 1930s, were every bit as real to their admirers as any living personage. Ever since Palmer Cox allowed his Brownies to be sold as rag dolls in 1891, children's artists—including Rose O'Neill (section 28) and Grace Drayton (section 29)—have provided inspiration for the creation of dolls from Raggedy Ann to Uncle Wiggly. Ever since R. F. Outcault created the first comic-strip characters of the 1890s—the Yellow Kid, Happy Hooligan, Buster Brown—there has existed a symbiotic love affair between cartoonist, doll manufacturer, and an adoring public. It is no exaggeration to suggest that virtually every major storybook, comic strip, and cartoon character has been marketed as a doll or dolls. (The marketing genius of Walt Disney alone has been the subject of several full-length books for collectors.)

24-O Barney Google and Spark Plug (color plate)
Probably A. Schoenhut & Co.
Philadelphia, Pennsylvania, 1922
7¼" (Barney Google)
8" tall by 9½" long (Spark Plug)

All-wood dolls. Barney Google jointed at neck, shoulders, hips, and feet. Decal at bottom of left foot obliterated. Spark Plug is jointed at neck, shoulders, legs, and hooves. Ears are leather. On felt blanket: "SPARK//PLUG". Decal on bottom of body: "Copyright 1922 by//King Features Inc.//Patent Applied For". [Barney Google and Spark Plug were the creations of cartoonist Billy DeBeck.] **(Pair, C)**

24-1 Mutt and Jeff
A. Bucherer
Amriswil, Switzerland, c. 1921
8" (Mutt), 6½" (Jeff)

Ball-jointed metal dolls with composition heads, hands, and shoes; original felt clothing. Incised on bodies: "MADE IN//SWITZERLAND//PATENTS//APPLIED FOR". [For illustration of how dolls are jointed, see 13-7.] **(Pair, C)**

24-2 Maggie and Jiggs (left and right)
Probably A. Schoenhut & Co.
Philadelphia, Pennsylvania, 1924
8½" (Maggie), 7" (Jiggs)

All-wood dolls, jointed at neck, shoulders, hips, and ankles. Decals at bottom of left feet obliterated. [Based on the comic-strip characters created by George McManus in **Bringing Up Father** and trademarked and distributed by George Borgfeldt. A lunch pail for Jiggs and a rolling pin for Maggie could be bought separately for insertion in their clothespin-like hands.] **(B)**

Felix the Cat (center)
Probably A. Schoenhut & Co.
Philadelphia, Pennsylvania, 1924
4"

Wooden doll, jointed at neck, shoulders, hips, feet, and tail; tail itself is jointed in 10 places; leather ears. Decal on chest: "FELIX". Decal on bottom of left foot: "FELIX//COPYRIGHT 1922, 1924 BY//PAT. SULLIVAN// PAT. APPLIED FOR". [Like the character created by cartoonist Pat Sullivan, this doll could balance itself by its tail. Also available in 8½" size. Distributed by George Borgfeldt.] **(D)**

24-3 Ella Cinders
E.I. Horsman & Aetna Doll Co.
New York City, c. 1925
18"

Composition head on cloth body
with composition arms and legs;
molded and painted features
and hair; flange neck, jointed at
shoulders and hips. Embossed on
back of head: "©//1925//M.N.S."
(D)

24-4 Skippy
EFFanBEE
New York City, c. 1930
14"

Composition head, body, and
limbs; molded and painted features and hair; swivel neck, jointed
at shoulders and hips. Embossed
on back of head: "EFFANBEE//SKIP-
PY//©//P.L. Crosby [in script]". Embossed on back of body: "EFFAN-
BEE // PATSY // PATENTED // DOLL".
[Made at the height of the Patsy
craze, Skippy heads were frequently sold on Patsy bodies. P.L.
Crosby was the cartoonist who
created Skippy.] **(E)**

24-5 Three Early Mickey and Minnie Mouse Dolls
Various Makers
American, 1926-33

Micky [sic] (left)
Maker unidentified, after 1926
4½"

Wooden doll with cloth-covered wire tail, arms, and legs. Label on body: "MICKY". Label on bottom of left foot: "MICKY TRADE MARK//Reg. U.S. Pat. Off.//Pat. Aug 17. 1926". [The misspelling of Mickey and the patent date are probably deliberate attempt to circumvent Walt Disney's copyright.] **(D)**

Minnie Mouse (center)
Butler Bros.
New York City, c. 1933
3⅞"

Turned-wood doll with wire arms, legs, and tail, leather ears; swivels at neck and waist. Decal on body: MINNIE//MOUSE//COPR. (obliterated)// WALT E. DISNEY". [Also available in 5⅛" size.] **(D)**

Mickey Mouse (right)
Maker Unconfirmed (?)
Akron, Ohio, c. 1933
3½"

Molded rubber doll; painted features. Embossed on back: © WALT DISNEY//BETBERLING LATEX//MADE IN AKRON O. U.S.A." **(D)**

24-6 Betty Boop
Designed by Joseph L. Kallus
Cameo Doll Co.
Port Allegany, Pennsylvania
1932
12"

All-composition doll; molded and painted features and hair; swivel neck, jointed at shoulders, elbows, wrists, and hips. Heart-shaped decal on chest: "'BETTY-BOOP'//DES & COPYRIGHT//BY FLEISCHER//STUDIOS". [Betty Boop was the creation of movie cartoonist Max Fleischer. Although the doll illustrated is wearing its original dress, another model came with a red molded composition dress in the somewhat sexy style affected by Betty Boop; the heart-shaped decal appeared on the dress itself in this second model.] **(D)**

24-7 Little Orphan Annie
Maker and place unknown
c. 1930s
10½"

Composition head, body, and limbs; molded and painted features and hair, (unlike the comic-strip Annie, the doll has eyeballs); jointed at shoulders and hips. [This doll was sometimes sold together with a composition "Sandy," Annie's dog. Photographed together with Orphan Annie shaker mug, an Ovaltine premium of 1940.] **(E)**

24-8 Little Orphan Annie
Stack Mfg. Co.

c. 1936
5"

Turned wood head, body, and limbs; painted features, brightly enameled body; elastic-strung moveable joints. Stamped on body: "LITTLE
ORPHAN ANNIE//HAROLD//GRAY—". [Photographed with a Little Orphan Annie toy range. Harold Gray, of course, was the creator of
Annie.] **(E)**

24-9 Snow White and the Seven Dwarfs
Knickerbocker Toy Co.
New York City, c. 1939
14½" (Snow White), 9" (Dwarfs)

Snow White: Composition head, body, and limbs; molded and
painted features and hair; swivel neck, jointed at shoulders and hips.
Embossed on back of head: "© WALT DISNEY". Embossed on back of
body: "KNICKERBOCKER TOY CO.//NEW YORK".

Dwarfs: One-piece composition head and body, composition arms
jointed at shoulders; molded and painted features, mohair beards on
all except Dopey; felt clothing, including hats which are marked with
names of Dwarfs: Happy, Bashful, Sleepy, Sneezy, Grumpy, Doc, and
Dopey; cloth glasses on Doc. Embossed on back of bodies: "© WALT
DISNEY//KNICKERBOCKER TOY CO." **(Entire set, C)**

24-10 Sparkle Plenty (left)
Ideal Toy Corporation
New York City, c. 1947
15"

"Magic Skin" doll, molded and painted features and hair, sleeping eyes and lashes, yarn hair wig glued on top of molded hair. Embossed on back of head: "MADE IN USA [and patent number]." [In the late 1940s, Sparkle Plenty was the infant daughter of B.O. Plenty and Gravel Gertie in Chester Gould's comic strip, **Dick Tracy**.] **(E)**

Bonnie Braids Toddler (center)
Ideal Toy Corporation
New York City, 1951
13"

Soft vinyl head on hard plastic walker body; open-closed mouth with three upper teeth, sleeping eyes, molded and painted hair with Saran braids; swivel neck, jointed at shoulders and hips. Embossed on back of head: "COPR 1951//IDEAL DOLL//U.S.A." Embossed on back of body: "IDEAL DOLL//14". [After an engagement of close to 20 years, comic strip gumshoe Dick Tracy finally married Tess Trueheart and produced Bonnie Braids before both rusted.] **(E)**

Joan Palooka (right)
Ideal Toy Corporation
New York City, 1952
13½"

All-vinyl unjointed doll; open-closed mouth with tongue, sleeping eyes with lashes, molded and painted hair with tuft of synthetic hair at top. Embossed on back of head: "©//HAM FISHER//IDEAL DOLL". Label says, among other things, "Smells like a real baby, fresh from her bath with appealing Johnson's Baby Powder fragrance." [Joan Palooka was the daughter of Ham Fisher's prize-fighting comic-strip character, Joe Palooka, and his wife, Ann, who, upon presenting her new-born daughter to her husband, uttered the immortal words: "Tee Hee."] **(E)**

25 | Bonnet Dolls

Simply put, any doll's head having a **molded** bonnet, cap, or other form of hat is called a "bonnet doll." Bonnet dolls were made in several materials, including china (25-0), wax over composition (25-1), bisque (25-4), parian (25-5), and especially stone bisque (25-2, 25-3)—a nontranslucent type of bisque. Stone bisque bonnet dolls enjoyed a vogue during the early 1900s, the headdresses occasionally molded as fanciful butterflies or flowers. Waxed bonnet dolls—very much like pumpkin heads with hats—often feature flat hats with stiff feathers, all of course molded in the wax. These hats are generally placed at the back of the head, a position not requiring more than the two- or three-piece molds generally used in making standard waxed pumpkin heads. Occasionally, waxed bonnet dolls have mohair glued to the head just beneath the brim of the hat, a realistic touch that somehow detracts from the doll's overall appearance. Bonneted half-dolls (pincushion dolls) are pictured in section 34.

25-O Bonnet Doll (color plate)
Maker unidentified
German, late 19th century
14" (entire doll), 3½" (shoulder head)

China shoulder head, cloth body with bisque hands; molded and painted features and blonde hair, molded yellow bonnet with blue ribbon; jointed at shoulders and hips. Incised on back of shoulder plate: "9" **(E)**

25-1 Waxed Bonnet Doll
Maker unidentified
German, 19th century
10½" (entire doll)
4" (shoulder head)

Wax over composition shoulder head, molded and painted features, glass pupil-less eyes, hair glued to head; wax bonnet with red and pink plume; cloth body with wooden arms and legs, blue wooden boots. **(D)**

25-2 Marguerite Doll (Butterfly Doll)
Possibly Hamburger & Co.
Berlin, c. 1902
10"

Stone Bisque shoulder head with butterly hood in pale blue with red spots; molded and painted features and blonde hair, glazed gilt bow at bodice; cloth body with china limbs, blue-painted stockings, ivory-painted shoes with orange-painted ribbons. **(D)**

25-3 Bonnet Doll
Possibly Butler Bros.
Sonneberg, Thür., c. 1905
11" (entire doll)
3" (shoulder head)

Stone Bisque shoulder head with blue bonnet; molded and painted features and blonde hair, molded bodice with glazed gilt ribbon; cloth body with bisque forearms; jointed at shoulders, hips, and knees. Incised on back of breast plate: "0". **(E)**

25-4 Bonnet Character Babies
Probably Th. Recknagel
Alexandrinenthal, Thür., c. 1912
9" (each)

Bisque heads with molded bonnets (girl's with glazed pink ribbon and bow); composition bent-limb baby bodies; open-closed mouths with two painted upper teeth, intaglio eyes; swivel necks, jointed at shoulders and hips. Incised on back of head: "28-7/0" (boy) and "29-7/0" (girl). **(Each, D)**

25-5 Modern Bonnet Doll
Emma C. Clear
Los Angeles, California, 1940
15"

Untinted bisque shoulder head with bonnet on cloth body with china lower limbs; molded and painted features, blonde painted hair; jointed at shoulders, hips, and knees. Incised on back of breast plate: "40 Clear". **(D)**

26 | Advertising and Premium Dolls

The age of modern advertising in America began with the introduction of Rural Free Delivery by the federal government in 1896, an innovation that made possible such catalogue houses as Sears, Roebuck and Montgomery Ward (both of which sold enormous quantities of dolls) and also spawned an entirely new idea: premium advertising, by which a manufacturer could increase sales of a product substantially by giving away a free gift. Producers of breakfast cereal in particular were quick to learn that an inexpensive rag doll, offered in exchange for several box tops and a small fee "for postage and handling" could boost sales dramatically, a lesson that has held them in good stead for eighty years, even if the small fee, and the premium itself, have changed over the years. Among the first of the advertising dolls to appear was Sunny Jim, offered to the contented consumers of Force breakfast cereal in 1905. Other breakfast cereal dolls are illustrated in the pages that follow, together with dolls for such household products as Fels-Naptha soap. Advertising dolls add an unabashedly nostalgic touch to any collection for a very moderate price and are more than worth their weight in unpretentious charm.

26-O Rastus, the Cream of Wheat Chef (color plate)
Maker unidentified
American, 1930
18" (excluding hat)

Cutout printed cloth doll with lithographed features, arms, clothing. Created to promote popular breakfast cereal. On lithographed bowl: "CREAM OF WHEAT". **(F)**

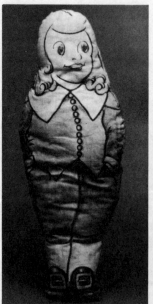

26-1 Quaker Crackels Boy
Maker unidentified

American, c. 1910
15½"

Cutout printed cloth doll, resembling Little Lord Fauntleroy, made to promote a breakfast cereal. In back pocket of trousers is a lithographed box of Quaker Crackels. **(F)**

26-2 Premium Doll

Art Fabric Mills
New York City, c. 1905
23"

Cutout printed rag doll with blue
hair ribbon, underwear with blue
ribbon, and yellow high-button
shoes, all lithographed. Printed on
bottom of right foot: "FEB. 13,
1900". [This doll was given free by
Cook's Flaked Rice Company with
a coupon from the cereal package and ten cents to cover mail-
ing costs.] **(F)**

26-4 Aunt Jemima
Aunt Jemima Mills Co.
St. Joseph, Missouri, c. 1925
14½"

Cutout printed rag doll with lithographed features, arms, and yellow, black, and red clothing. Printed on red-and-white striped ap-
ron: "Aunt Jemima". [Redesigned
version of the 1908 doll, originally
sold for 25¢ plus a box top from
Aunt Jemima Pancake Flour.] **(F)**

26-3 Anty Drudge
Maker unidentified
American, c. 1910
10"

Cutout printed cloth doll with lithographed features, arms, clothing.
Made to promote Fels-Naptha
soap. Doll carries a lithographed
package of Fels-Naptha soap.
Pattern on dress repeats the words
"Fels-Naptha Soap." **(F)**

26-5 Uncle Mose, Wade Davis, and Diana
Aunt Jemima Mills Co.
St. Joseph, Missouri, c. 1925
15" (Uncle Mose), 12" (Wade Davis and Diana)

Cutout printed rag dolls with lithographed features, arms, and red, yellow, and blue clothing. Uncle Mose holds a pipe; Wade Davis, his hat; and Diana, a cat. Printed on back of dolls: "Uncle Mose//AUNT JEMIMA'S//HUSBAND"; "Wade//AUNT JEMIMA'S LITTLE BOY"; "Diana//AUNT JEMIMA'S//LITTLE GIRL". [Aunt Jemima and her family had been made into rag dolls as early as 1908; they were originally sold for 25¢ plus a box top from Aunt Jemima Pancake Flour. The dolls pictured here are the redesigned set of the 1920s.] **(Each, F)**

26-6 Buddy Lee
Made for H.D. Lee Mercantile Co.
San Francisco, California
1920-25
13"

All-composition doll; molded and painted features and hair, jointed at shoulders only. Label on cap: "UNION MADE//Lee//SANFORIZED// SHRUNK". Same label on back of overalls. [Doll was used each year, in different Lee work outfits and playsuits, as part of a window display and then sold to the public as a doll after its display use.] **(E)**

27 | Multi-face, Multi-head, and Topsy-turvy Dolls

Multi-face, multi-head, and topsy-turvy dolls—three distinctively different types of playthings—have one element in common: an attempt to give more than one fixed expression to a single doll. Multi-face dolls generally have two-, three-, or four-faced heads that rotate on a vertical axis. Two-faced dolls very frequently have one white and one black face. Three-faced dolls usually have features that are sleeping, laughing, and crying. Multi-face dolls were made of virtually every material—papier-mâché, wax, bisque, rubber and rag—from the 1860s through the early 20th century.

Multi-head dolls featured sets of detachable heads that could be screwed to a doll's body at will, changing its personality in an instant. The "Five-in-One" doll, for example, had five interchangeable celluloid heads and could readily be turned into a boy, a girl, and even a cat! The topsy-turvy doll is simply another form of multi-head doll in which two half-dolls are joined at the waist. When one head is revealed, the other is concealed by clothing. Although topsy-turvy dolls are known to have bisque heads, most found today are the well-known "Topsy and Eva" rag dolls with one black and one white head.

27-0 Three-faced Doll (color plate)
Probably Carl Bergner
Sonneberg, Thür., c. 1911
9"

Three-faced bisque head (laughing, crying, sleeping) on composition bent-limb baby body; head surrounded by papier-mâché hood with attached hair that frames selected face; ring at top for turning head. Stamped on back: [within circle] "C.B." **(C)**

27-1 The Famlee Doll (Multi-face Doll)
European Doll Mfg. Co.
New York City, c. 1920s
16" (each head, 4½")

Composition heads with molded and painted features and human or molded hair, cloth body with composition forearms and lower legs; jointed at shoulders and hips; voice box. [Heads screw on to breast plate.] **(D)**

27-2 Trudy (Sleepy, Weepy, Smily)
Designed by Elsie Gilbert
The Three-In-One Doll Corp.
New York City, 1946
14½"

Three-faced bisque head, cloth body and limbs; molded and painted features, synthetic hair attached to hood. Printed label: "An Elsie Gilbert Creation [in script]// PATENTS PENDING//TRUDY//TRADE-MARK OF THE//THREE-IN-ONE DOLL// CORP.// [handwritten serial number]". [Knob at top turns head to desired face.] **(F)**

27-3 Topsy-Turvy Doll
Fan Sieber
American, contemporary
12½"

An exquisite modern version of the traditional (and rare) topsy-turvy doll, employing bisque shoulder heads and arms on a single cloth trunk. **(F)**

28 | Kewpies and Other Rose O'Neill Dolls

Rose O'Neill's whimsical line drawings of fairy-like Kewpies first appeared in the **Ladies Home Journal** in 1909, accompanied by her excruciating verse. Both were immediately popular with adults, as was the long line of Kewpie dolls that followed in 1912. The idea for a Kewpie doll was Rose O'Neill's, although her handmade rag doll was rejected by George Borgfeldt in favor of an O'Neill-designed bisque, first made at the Kestner factory in Germany. Joseph Kallus supervised both the modeling and the initial manufacturing of the impish figures with blue wings. The success of these dolls was immediate, and, like the original O'Neill drawings, their appeal was particularly to adults who demanded (and got) Kewpie figures of every size and form in the years to come. By the beginning of World War I, some twenty-one factories in Germany and the United States were manufacturing bisque and composition Kewpies to meet the demand of the American market alone. Black Kewpies, later called Hottentots, were introduced in 1914 and had white wings instead of the standard blue. Eventually, Kewpies were modeled in every sort of costume—fireman, policeman, soldier, musician—and some, called "instructive Kewpies," engaged in such social activities as sharing a book. Scootles, a later O'Neill doll also created in collaboration with Joseph Kallus, never achieved the popularity of the Kewpie.

28-O Composition Kewpie (color plate)
Designed by Rose O'Neill
Probably Cameo Doll Company
New York City, c. 1922
11"

All-composition doll; molded and painted features and hair; jointed at shoulders; blue molded and painted wings at rear. Red heart-shaped decal: "KEWPIE//DES. & COPYRIGHT//by//ROSE O'NEILL". [Decal phrasing identical to that preferred by Joseph Kallus's Cameo Doll Company.] **(E)**

28-1 All-Bisque Kewpies
Various manufacturers, 1912-1920s
Sizes range from 2" to 7"

Photograph shows size range of miniature Kewpies and their variety:
legs together, legs apart, jointed legs, unjointed legs, eyes to left, eyes
to right, etc. One doll (second from left) has heart-shaped decal
("KEWPIE//Germany"). **(Each, E)**

28-2 All-Composition Kewpie (left)
Designed by Rose O'Neill
Specific maker unidentified, probably 1920s
12½"

All-composition doll, jointed at shoulders; pale-blue wings on back,
blue base. Heart-shaped decal: "KEWPIE//DESIGN PAT//NO. 4360//REG
U.S.//PAT OFF". Label on underside of base: "© ROSE O'NEILL 1913". **(E)**

Cloth Kewpie (right)
Maker and place unidentified
c. 1920s-1930s
22"

Composition head on cloth body; molded and painted features;
flange neck, jointed at shoulders and hips. Unmarked. **(F)**

28-3 Hottentot
Designed by Rose O'Neill
Probably Cameo Doll Company
New York City, c. 1922
14"

All-composition doll, jointed at
shoulders; molded and painted
features and hair, molded red
wings on back. Heart-shaped decal on chest: "KEWPIE//DES. &
COPYRIGHT/by//ROSE O'NEILL".
[Although black Kewpies were first
made in 1914, they were named
"Hottentots" a year later.] **(E)**

28-4 Contemporary Kewpie
Cameo Doll Co.
Port Allegany, Pennsylvania
1960s
12"

All-vinyl doll; swivel neck, jointed
at shoulders and hips. Incised on
back of head: "CAMEO ©". Label: "CAMEO ART QUALITY DOLLS."
Reverse side: [printed over draw-
ing of Kewpie] 'KEWPIE'//BRAND
DOLL//originally//DESIGNED
AND//COPYRIGHT BY// [facsimile of

28-5 Black Scootles
Designed by Rose O'Neill
Cameo Doll Co.
Port Allegany, Pennsylvania
1930s

All-composition doll; molded and
painted features and hair; swivel
neck, jointed at shoulders and

hips. [Scootles was first made of bisque in 1925; the word "Scootles" was incised on bottom of foot. Black Scootles are rare.] **(E)**

Rose O'Neill's signature]//A//CAMEO DOLL". [Manufactured by Joseph Kallus who holds Kewpie copyright.] **(F)**

---

29 | Campbell Kids and Other Grace Drayton Dolls

As the Colemans observe, there are striking similarities between drawings of the American artists Grace Drayton and Rose O'Neill—"the round faces and eyes, the single curved line of the mouth with lines at the corners, and the starfish-shaped hands." Both were among the first American illustrators to produce popular drawings upon which equally popular dolls were based. Grace Drayton's best-known creations, the Campbell Kids, introduced in advertisements for the Campbell Soup Co. in 1900, obscure her other successes, notably the **Bobby and Dolly** series of books that sold some 200,000 copies by 1911. Dolls made in imitation of the Campbell Kids were made by Horsman as early as 1910. Although such dolls are marked "E.I.H. ©1910," no such copyright was ever recorded; Grace Drayton's own involvement in the dolls' production is also in question since the Campbell Soup Co. held the copyright on her drawings for them. The artist's own involvement in the design of Louis Amberg's Bobby Blake doll is even more doubtful. Although she did give Amberg permission to base the doll on her character, and no doubt profited from her consent, the actual doll was designed by artist Helen Trowbridge. In examining Drayton dolls, however, one trait is not at all in doubt: it is perfectly clear why goo-goo eyes are sometimes called "Drayton eyes."

29-0 Original Campbell Kids (color plate)
Designed by Grace Drayton
E.I. Horsman Co.
New York City, c. 1910
12" (boy), 11¾" (girl)

Composition heads on cloth bodies with composition hands; molded and painted features, painted hair; jointed at shoulders, hips, and wrists; original clothing. Embossed on back of heads: "E.I.H. © 1910". **(Pair, D)**

29-1 Campbell Kid
Designed by Grace Drayton
E.I. Horsman Co.
New York City, c. 1910
9"

Composition head on cloth body; painted and molded features, painted hair, jointed at shoulders and hips. Embossed on back of head: "E.I.H. © 1910". **(E)**

29-2 Shoulder-Head Bobby Blake
Designed by Grace Drayton
Louis Amberg & Son
New York City, after 1911
13½" (entire doll), 4½" (shoulder head)

Composition shoulder head on cloth body with composition limbs;

molded and painted features and hair; jointed at shoulders and hips. Embossed on back of head: "G.G. Drayton [in script]//©". [The first Bobby Blake dolls were made in 1911. They had composition heads and hands and a cork-stuffed body.] **(E)**

29-3 The Gee-Gee Dolly
Designed by Grace Drayton
E.I. Horsman Co.
New York City, 1912-14
8"

All-composition doll, jointed at shoulders; molded and painted features. Unmarked. [**Playthings** for April 1913 reports that "The Gee-Gees are indestructible dolls with flatish, moon-shaped faces, merry upturned mouths, cute 'snub noses' and wide open, laughing eyes."] **(E)**

30 | Boudoir Dolls

The famous French couturier Paul Poiret set the tone in 1910: fashionable women were to carry dolls. Elegantly dressed dolls, wearing fashions by Poiret, Lanvin, and Paquin, became the vogue among the **haute monde,** and, like any other fad, the fashion eventually passed down to the middle classes before dying out. But the idea of dolls for adult women persisted through the 1920s. Although the better-made French "mascots" were taken motoring by their wealthy owners, their cheaper counterparts—the cloth "flappers" with Charleston dresses revealing long, thin legs and high-heeled shoes—were taken to tea dances at cheap chop-suey joints by more ordinary women. By the time the faintly absurd fad abated, the dolls were kept at home, on beds or dressing tables; hence their generic name—boudoir dolls. Boudoir dolls, not highly regarded by today's connoisseurs, are collectibles of tomorrow. With prices still comparatively low, they should prove an attractive investment in the future.

30-O Boudoir Doll (color plate)
Maker and place unidentified
c. 1930
24" (entire doll), 8" (shoulder head)

Composition shoulder head on cloth body with composition arms and lower legs with high-heeled shoes; molded and painted features, mohair wig; jointed at shoulders and hips; original clothing. **(F)**

30-1 Wax Boudoir Doll
Maker unidentified
Probably French, c. 1925-30
20"

Wax shoulder head on cloth body, wax arms and legs joined to body by cork blocks; molded and painted features, human hair wig; wax high-heeled shoes; original silk clothing. **(E)**

30-2 French Flapper
N.V. Sales Company
New York City, c. 1925
24½"

Composition head, body, and limbs; molded and painted fea-

tures, composition cigarette, red human hair wig; swivel neck, fully jointed (except wrists); original felt trouser suit and high-heeled shoes. **(E)**

30-3 Boudoir Doll
Maker and place unidentified
c. 1930
22" (entire doll)
7" (shoulder head)

Composition shoulder head on cloth body with composition arms and legs with molded high-heeled shoes; molded and painted features, mohair wig; jointed at shoulders and hips; original clothing. **(F)**

30-4 Boudoir Doll
Maker and place unidentified
c. 1930
26"

Composition head on pink cloth body; molded and painted features, human hair wig; jointed at shoulders and hips. **(F)**

31 | Dolls' House Dolls and Other Miniatures

There is no end to the fascinating variety of small dolls made for use in dolls' houses, simple play, or decorative display. Such dolls have been made of virtually every material, but those of bisque (whether all-bisque or bisque shoulder heads with cloth bodies and bisque lower limbs) seem best to capture the essence of dolls' house families commercially made in Germany and France in the late 19th and early 20th centuries. Even the most humble dolls' houses seemed to have had a butler and maid attending the family: mother, father, grandparents, and children (usually one boy and one girl). Although such firms as Heinrich Schmuckler specialized in "fine dressed dolls for doll rooms," most small dolls are unmarked, their makers being almost completely unknown and their dates cautiously approximated by the style of their clothing. Because the wide universe of dolls' house dolls and miniatures can only be suggested here, the collector seeking comprehensive information should begin with **Inside the World of Miniatures and Dollhouses** by Bernard Rosner and Jay Beckerman.

31-O Doll's House Dolls (color plate)
Makers and place unidentified
Probably German, early 20th century
4" (children), 5½" (butcher)

Three all-bisque dolls—children with glass eyes and human hair, butcher with molded and painted features and hair—jointed at shoulders and hips. [Photographed against a mid-19th-century carved and painted replica of an English butcher shop.] **(Each doll, F)**

31-1 Miniature Bisque-Head Dolls
Possibly Th. Recknagel
Alexandrinenthal, Germany, 1907

7" (each)

Bisque heads, composition bodies and limbs; open-closed mouths, two upper teeth, glass sleeping eyes, human hair wigs; jointed at shoulders and hips; painted shoes and stockings. Marked on back of heads: "1907// R/A // DEP // L 14". **(Each, E)**

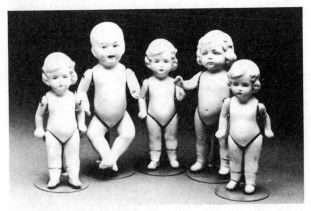

31-2 Miniature All-Bisque Dolls
Limbach Porzellanfabrik
Limbach, Thür., c. 1920s
Sizes range from 4" to 4½"

All-bisque dolls, jointed at shoulders and hips. Incised on back: "[three-leaf clover]//MADE IN GERMANY". **(Each, F)**

31-3 Miniatures
Makers unidentified
German, 1920s
Left to right: 4½", 5", 3½", 4"

Two boys at left have nodding painted-bisque heads on solid-bisque bodies; each incised "Germany" on back. Seated all-bisque doll is jointed at shoulders and hips; molded and painted face. Nodder at right is comic-strip character Andy Gump; incised on back: "ANDY// GUMP// Germany." **(Each, F)**

31-4 Miniatures
Makers unidentified
Sizes range from ¾" to 2"

Baby in real walnut shell is marked "MADE IN FRANCE." To its left is a miniature Happy Hooligan doll. At bottom left is a miniature beefeater, and at bottom center are miniature Raggedy Ann and Andy dolls. **(Each, F)**

31-5 Assorted Miniatures
Makers unidentified, 1920s-30s
Sizes range from 2" to 3½"

Top row from left to right: two bisque doll's house dolls, Frozen Charlotte, rubber doll in knitted outfit. Lower right: Frozen Charlotte, two stone bisque dolls from Japan, Japanese china doll, the Dionne Quintuplets with wooden heads. **(Each, F)**

31-6 Doll's House Couple (left and center)
Maker and place unidentified

Early 20th century
7½" (each doll), 2" (each shoulder head)

Bisque shoulder heads, cloth bodies with bisque forearms and legs with molded shoes; molded and painted features; molded and painted hair and beard (man), human hair wig (woman). Unmarked. **(Each, E)**

Miniature China-Limb Doll (right)
Maker unidentified
German, late 19th or early 20th century
7" (entire doll), 2" (shoulder head)

China shoulder head on cloth body with china arms and china legs with molded shoes; molded and painted features and hair. Unmarked. **(E)**

31-7 Doll's House Dolls
Makers unidentified
Probably German, c. 1920
Sizes range from 4" to 5"

All-bisque dolls; molded and painted features and hair; jointed at shoulders and hips. **(Each, E)**

32 | Foreign Costume Dolls

Dolls dressed in native costumes of foreign countries have always been popular. Long before the educational phrase "visual aids" was ever coined, foreign costume dolls were used as an aid in teaching geography to children. They were also favorite gifts from friends and relatives who had returned from travels abroad, with many girls devoting a corner of their rooms to souvenir dolls from all over the globe. Most of these dolls were made in Germany and exported to natives of other countries who dressed them in national garb and sold them to tourists. So great was their number that many of the re-dressed antique dolls sold today were in fact originally foreign costume dolls.

32-O Oriental Character Baby (color plate)
J.D. Kestner, Jr.
Waltershausen, Thür., after 1909
15"

Yellow-tinted bisque head on composition bent-limb baby body; open mouth with two upper teeth, almond-shaped brown glass sleeping eyes, human hair wig; swivel neck, jointed at shoulders and hips; original clothing. Wig obscures mark on back of head which is probably: "Made in Germany [script]//243//J.D.K." **(B)**

32-1 Oriental Toddler (left)
König & Wernicke
Waltershausen, Thür., after 1912
14½"

J.D. Kestner olive-tinted bisque head on yellow-tinted composition bent-limb body; open mouth with two upper teeth, almond-shaped brown glass sleeping eyes, human hair wig; swivel neck, jointed at shoulders and hips; original clothing. Incised on back of head: "164". Stamped on body: "[within circle] Made in Germany//K & W". **(B)**

Oriental Child (right)

Maker unconfirmed
Germany, after 1909
8"

Tinted bisque head, composition bent-limb baby body; closed mouth, almond-shaped brown glass sleeping eyes, painted hair; swivel neck, jointed at shoulders and hips. Incised on back of head: "5/0//Germany". [This doll was very likely made by Armand Marseille.] **(C)**

32-3 English Beefeater
Gebrüder Heubach
Lichte, Thür., early 20th century
14" (including hat)

Bisque shoulder head on cloth body with composition forearms; closed mouth, intaglio eyes, molded hair; jointed at shoulders. Incised on back of shoulder plate, "O". (Original clothing, sewn shut, obscures remainder of mark.) [Doll was probably made at time of coronation of George V in 1910.] **(E)**

32-2 Oriental Lady Doll
Shoenau & Hoffmeister
Burggrub, Bavaria, after 1901
18½" (including wig)

Yellow-tinted bisque head, composition body and limbs; open mouth with four upper teeth, brown almond-shaped glass eyes, human hair wig; swivel neck, fully jointed; original clothing. Incised on back of head; "S [five-pointed star marked 'PB'] H". [The "PB" stands for "Porzellanfabrik Burggrub," i.e., "Burggrub Porcelain Factory."] **(C)**

32-4 Spanish Señorita (left)
Maker and place unidentified
c. 1920
9¾"

Cloth body with stockinet-over-mask head; molded and painted features, glass eyes, mohair wig; metal joints at shoulders and hips. **(F)**

Dutch Woman (center)
Maker and place unidentified
c. 1920s
10½"

Composition shoulder head on cloth body with wooden shoes; molded and painted features, human hair wig; jointed at shoulders and hips. **(F)**

Bavarian Boy (right)
Maker unidentified
German, c. 1920
8"

Bisque head on cloth body; molded and painted features, human hair wig; jointed at shoulders and hips. Incised on back of head: "Germany". **(F)**

32-5 Scottish Boy
Maker unidentified
German, late 19th century
10" (entire doll)
3" (shoulder head)

Untinted bisque shoulder head, cloth body, bisque forearms, legs, and boots; closed mouth, intaglio eyes, blonde molded and painted hair; jointed at shoulders and hips. Incised on back of shoulder plate: "1222—3/0". **(E)**

32-6 Scottish Highlander
Maker and place unidentified
c. 1920
13"

Composition head on cloth body;
molded and painted features
and hair; flange neck, jointed at
shoulders and hips. **(F)**

32-7

32-7 Dutch Boy (left)
Ernst Heubach
Köppelsdorf, Thür., early 20th century
8"

Painted bisque head, composition body; open mouth with four upper teeth, glass sleeping eyes, human hair wig; swivel neck, jointed at shoulders and hips; wooden shoes. Incised on back of head: "Heubach-Köppelsdorf//251.7/0//Germany". **(F)**

Dutch Girl (right)
Maker unidentified
Probably German, early 20th century
10"

Composition shoulder head on cloth body; molded and painted features, human hair wig over molded hair; jointed at shoulders and hips; wooden shoes. **(F)**

32-8 Dutch Boy and Girl
Maker unidentified
Probably German, c. 1920
12" (each)

Painted bisque shoulder heads on cloth bodies with composition arms and legs with wooden shoes; molded and painted features and hair (girl has mohair glued to front of head over molded hair); jointed at shoulders and hips. **(Each, F)**

32-9 Oriental Boy (left)
Maker and place unidentified
1930s
11″

All-composition doll; molded and painted features; swivel head, jointed at shoulders and hips. Unmarked. **(F)**

Eskimo (right)
Pullan Doll Co.
Canadian, c. 1930
14″

All-composition doll; molded and painted features and hair; swivel neck, jointed at shoulders and hips; original costume. Embossed on back of body: "A PULLAN DOLL". [Doll is believed by some collectors to have been created to commemorate The Cliquot Club Esquimos, an early radio orchestra sponsored by a carbonated beverage company. Given the great interest in Polar exploration by airplane and dirigible during the '20s and '30s, such an explanation, without proof, seems far-fetched. **(F)**

33 | Black Dolls

One of the fastest-growing specialties of doll collecting is the appreciation of antique dolls representing blacks. This is the result not only of a contemporary interest in black history, but in the recognition that some of the most handsome bisque dolls ever made were delicately tinted to simulate the many shades of brown and black in the Negro spectrum. (Kämmer & Reinhardt, for example, advertised heads in various shades of "black, brown, and mulatto.") Although there were of course exceptions that underscore the sorry history of the black in the West, most black dolls escaped the visciously distorted stereotypes accorded their representation in toys. Black dolls seem to have been manufactured for at least two purposes: as dolls **for** black children (most successful dolls were also produced in black versions), and as dolls **representing** blacks to white children (ranging from exquisite bisques to the stereotypical rag-doll Mammy.)

33-O Black Doll (color plate)
Maker unidentified
German, but dressed and sold in Jamaica, early 20th century
11½"

Bisque head, composition body with wooden arms and hands; open mouth with four upper teeth, brown glass sleeping eyes, horsehair wig; swivel neck, jointed at shoulders, elbows, wrists, and hips. Incised on back of head: "34-20". Marked in ink on cotton drawers: "Kingston//Jamaica". [It is possible that this German-headed doll was assembled and sold in Jamaica to the tourist trade.] **(E)**

33-1 Mulatto Bisque
Unis France
Paris, c. 1922
10"

Bisque head, composition body and limbs; open mouth with four upper teeth, brown glass eyes, human hair wig; swivel neck, jointed at shoulders and hips. Incised on back of head: [within oval] "UNIS//FRANCE"//[outside oval] "60". **(D)**

33-2 Black Bisque Girl
Heinrich Handwerck
Gotha, Thür., after 1905
15"

Simon & Halbig bisque head, composition body and limbs; open mouth with four upper teeth, brown glass eyes, pierced ears, human hair wig; swivel neck, fully jointed; original clothing. Incised on back of head: "SIMON & HALBIG//HEINRICH//Germany//HANDWERCK". **(C)**

33-3 Black My Dream Baby
Armand Marseille
Köppelsdorf, Thür., c. 1925
8"

Bisque head on composition bent-limb baby body; closed mouth, brown glass eyes, painted hair; swivel neck, jointed at shoulders and hips. Incised on back of head: "A.M.//Germany//341.12/0. K". **(E)**

33-4 Black Composition Doll
Maker and place unidentified
c. 1930
8"

Composition head on composition bent-limb baby body; molded and painted features, molded hair and yarn to simulate "pickaninny" pigtails; swivel neck, jointed at shoulders and hips. [Very similar to black Patsy Baby by EFFanBEE, but unmarked.] **(F)**

33-5 Black Nun
Maker unidentified
American, c. 1930
22"

Composition shoulder head on cloth body with composition forearms; open mouth with two upper teeth, metal and glass eyes; jointed at shoulders and hips. [Dressed in 1930 by nuns in an all-black convent in New York City.] **(E)**

33-6 Amosandra
Sun Rubber Co.
Barberton, Ohio, 1930s
7" (seated)

All-rubber bent-limb baby doll; molded and painted features and hair; swivel neck, jointed at shoulders. Embossed on back of head: "AMOSANDRA/COLUMBIA BROADCASTING". Embossed on back of body: "DESIGNED BY RUTH E. NEWTON//MFG. BY//THE SUN RUBBER CO.//BARBERTON, OHIO// [patent number]". Amosandra was the daughter of Amos on CBS's **Amos 'n' Andy**; the baby could "drink" from a toy bottle. **(F)**

33-7 Black Raggedy Ann
Based on design by John B. Gruelle
Handmade, contemporary
18"

Rag doll jointed at shoulders, elbows, hips, and knees; button eyes and yarn hair. **(F)**

34 | Novelties

Not every doll is easily categorized. Those that did not seem to fit a standard commercial mold, that were too "new," too "odd," too "original," too "different," were generally sold by the trade as "novelties." Certainly, the first Kewpies, the first Campbell Kids, the first bent-limb baby dolls must have seemed novel indeed before their great successes. On the pages that follow are a gallery of dolls that were novel in their time. Some, like the engaging Fingy Legs (34-4), required the owner's fingers to complete its anatomy; others, like the Prialytine dolls (34-1) and the HEbee-SHEbee (43-8), were cartoon-like caricatures of the human form; still others, like the French poupards (34-2, 34-3)—also called **marottes** and **folies**—were designed to imitate the splendors of the 18th century, so admired by the fashionably rich at the beginning of the 20th.

34-O Miss Columbia (color plate)
Maker and place unidentified
Probably German, c. 1893
24"

Bisque head on composition body; open mouth with four upper teeth, brown glass eyes, pierced ears, human hair wig; swivel neck, fully jointed. Incised on back of head: "13". On white kid band around waist: "Columbian Exposition 1893". [Probably redressed.] **(D)**

34-1 Prialytine Dolls
Maker unidentified
Paris, c. 1900

9" (each)

Painted bisque head, bisque body and limbs; molded and painted features and hair, painted shoes and stockings; swivel neck, jointed at shoulders and hips. Incised on back of head: "La Prialytine//Paris". [Holes through right fists might indicate that dolls once held some object, possibly a flag.] **(Each, D)**

34-2 Poupard
Maker unidentified
French, c. 1900
2½" shoulder head on 8" stick

Bisque shoulder head with closed mouth, glass eyes, pierced ears, human hair wig; original costume with bells. Incised on back of head: "3/0". [It is believed that such dolls were used as party favors at the dinners and balls of the European haute monde.] **(C)**

34-3 Poupard
S.F.B.J.
Paris, c. 1900
2" head on 4" papier-mâché base with 5½" stick

Bisque head with open-closed mouth and teeth, glass eyes, and human hair wig; original costume and bells. Incised on back of head: "S.F.B.J.//60//PARIS". **(C)**

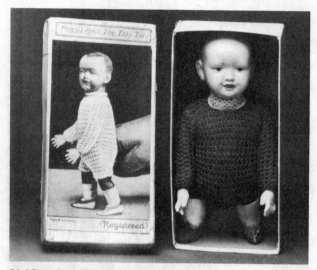

34-4 Fingy-Legs, The Tiny Tot
Rheinische Gummi und Celluloid Fabrik Co.
Mannheim-Neckarau, Bavaria, c. 1907
6½" (without feet)

Celluloid head and trunk, cloth arms, composition hands, composition feet (to be placed on finger tips); knitted suit. Embossed on back of head: "Germany [turtle mark] 8⅛". [This finger puppet, in which the fingers of the person holding it form the legs of the doll, was distributed in the U.S. by George Borgfeldt & Co. Photographed with original box.]
(E)

34-5 Matryushka (Nest of Wooden Dolls)
Maker unidentified
Russia, c. 1910
8" (assembled)

Nest of three wooden dolls (8", 5", 3½"), each divided in two halves, and each contained one within the other. Each doll represents a peasant woman in a babushka (kerchief). Features, arms, and babushka are crudely burned in wood. **(E)**

34-6 Whistling Clown
Maker unidentified
Probably German, c. 1913
12" (including hat)

Composition head and hat, wooden "bellows" trunk, cloth limbs; mouth puckered for "whistling"; painted features. [When squeezed, doll "whistles" and moves head from side to side. One of many dolls made to rival Gebrüder Heubach's bisque-headed "Whistling Jim."] **(E)**

34-7 Liberty Boy
Ideal Novelty & Toy Co.
New York City, 1918
12"

All-composition doll, jointed at neck, shoulders, and hips; molded uniform of an American soldier. Originally wore an Army felt hat with cord. **(E)**

34-8 HEbee-SHEbee
E.I. Horsman Co.
New York City, 1925
10½"

All-composition doll; painted features, molded clothing except yarn or ribbon shoelaces; swivel neck, jointed at shoulders and hips; white chemise and pink shoes; missing label at bottom of foot. [HEbees and SHEbees were modeled after the **Twelvetrees Kids**, drawn by Charles Twelvetrees. HEbees were identical to SHEbees, but wore blue shoes instead of pink. All-bisque HEbees-SHEbees came in 9" models. Dolls came dressed in various costumes, including a "Collegiate" outfit.] **(E)**

34-9 Comic Character
Maker and place unidentified
Early 20th century
6½"

All-papier-mâché doll; molded and painted features and painted clothing; swivel neck, jointed at shoulders and hips. [May possibly be based on Carl Schultze's comic strip "Foxy Grandpa."] **(F)**

34-10 Goo Goo Doll
Hermann Steiner
Sonneberg, Thür., c. 1925
12½"

Bisque head, cloth body and limbs; closed mouth, brown glass eyes with unattached pupils that move from side to side, molded and painted hair; flange neck, jointed at shoulders and hips. [Goo Goo eyes are also called "Flirting Eyes," "Goggle Eyes," "Eccentric Eyes," and "Roguish Eyes."] **(D)**

34-11 China Half-Dolls (two previous photographs)
Maker unidentified
German, 1920s
Sizes range from 2½" to 4½"

An assortment of china-half-dolls to be used as pincushion tops, tea cosy covers, brush covers, etc. Dressed either as modern flappers or as 18th-century ladies of fashion. Those with arms a distance away from torso are most valued by collectors. **(Each, E)**

34-12 Margie
Designed by Joseph Kallus
Cameo Doll Co.
New York City, 1929
10"

Composition head, wooden body and limbs; molded and painted features and hair; swivel neck constructed separately (not part of head), jointed at neck, shoulders, elbows, hips, knees, and ankles. [The first segmented wooden doll created by Joseph Kallus. Over 100,000 were sold in 1929 for 98¢ apiece.] **(E)**

34-13 Skookum Hopi Chief and Squaw with Papoose
Designed by Mary McAboy
Probably produced by H.H. Tammen Co.
Denver, Colorado and Los Angeles, California, c. 1920-38
23" (chief), 21" (squaw)

Composition head, cloth body and arms, wooden legs; molded and painted features, horsehair wig; not jointed. Original clothing, including leather leggings and woolen blanket. Hand-written label on bottom of left foot, indicating that dolls were purchased in California in 1938, obscures original Skookum trademark underneath. **(Each, D)**

34-14 Hotzi Notzi
Bassons Dummy Products
Maspeth, New York, 1941
5"

Plaster statuette of Adolf Hitler with pincushion derrière. Incised on base: "PAT PEND 1941. CPE". Paper label includes two mottoes: "IT IS GOOD LUCK TO FIND A PIN// HERE'S AN 'AXIS' TO STICK IT IN" and "HE WHO SEEKS TO STICK OTHERS— //HIMSELF GETS STUCK IN THE 'END'. [Novel spelling of Nazi probably because U.S. was not yet at war with Germany.] **(F)**

III SOME FAMOUS MAKERS

35 | Bru and Other Famous French Doll Makers

There is no denying that French dolls are among the most beautiful ever made. Yet it is a mistake to assume, as some collectors have, that every French doll is the **sine qua non** of artistry, superior to even the best German dolls. Although French dolls enjoyed a deserved reputation for excellence, many were made in fact with German and even English heads, and an equal number made during the early 20th century show signs of an artistic falling-off as a result of the losing battle with Germany for domination of the world doll market. "Competition" and "political history" are the operative words in generalizing about French doll production. Having enjoyed a reputation for fine dolls in the 17th and 18th centuries, France after the fall of the First Empire was forced to compete with England in the production of wax dolls and with Germany in that of china dolls. It is in the manufacture of fine bisque dolls, however, that France excelled in the thirty-year period following the Franco-Prussian War of 1870-1. The firms of Jumeau, Bru, Steiner, etc., produced bébés that were known worldwide for their exquisite beauty, fine workmanship, unsurpassed detail, and large glass eyes made very much like paperweights, but especially for their unexcelled kid bodies and modish French couturier-designed clothes. The French dolls illustrated in the following three sections suggest the range of French production during these years—from the treasured output of Bru and Jumeau to the decline of French genius in the face of German competition at the end of the 19th century.

35-O Bébé Teteur (Suckling Bru) (color plate)
Bru Jne. & Cie
Paris, 1881-98
18"

Bisque head and bosom on kid body with bisque forearms and wooden feet; open mouth, paperweight eyes, human hair wig; fully jointed; winding key in back of head. Incised on back of head: "BRU J^{NE}". Stamped "BRU" on shoulder plate. Label on bosom: "BÉBÉ BRU B^{TE} S.G.D.G.//Tout Contrafacteur sera saisi et poursuivi//conformément a la Loi." [Within the doll's head is a mechanism that enables the doll to "drink" its bottle. Patented by Casimir Bru, Jne., in 1879.] **(A)**

35-1 Closed-Mouth Bébé (Le Petit Parisien)
Jules Nicholas Steiner (also known as Société Steiner)
Paris, after 1889
21"

Bisque head, composition body and limbs; closed mouth, paperweight eyes, pierced ears, human hair wig; swivel neck, fully jointed. Incised on back of head: "J. STEINER//S^{TE} SGDG//PARIS//F1^{AE} A13". Label on thigh: [Picture of doll holding French flag in red, white, and blue, with the following on flag:] "Marque Déposée. LE PETIT PARISIEN//BÉBÉ J. STEINER". On label: "MEDAILLE D'OR//PARIS// 1889". **(B)**

35-2 Crying Jules Nicholas Steiner Doll
Jules Nicholas Steiner
Paris, c. 1880-90
20"

Bisque head, papier-mâché torso with composition arms and lower legs; open mouth with many upper and lower teeth, glass eyes, human hair wig. [When wound, clockwork mechanism causes doll to make crying sound and to kick arms and legs and move head from side to side] **(B)**

35-3 Unmarked Steiner Doll Attributed to Jules Nicholas Steiner
Paris, late 19th century

Bisque head, composition body and limbs; open-closed mouth, brown glass sleeping eyes, human hair wig, swivel neck, fully jointed body; original clothing. Incised on back of head: "15". [Doll attributed as French by Dorothy Coleman and as a Steiner by Doris Hupp.] **(B)**

35-4

35-4 Gaultier Shoulder-Head Doll
F. Gaultier
Paris, late 19th century

**11" (entire doll)
2½" (shoulder head)**

Bisque shoulder head on kid body; closed mouth, molded and painted features and hair; jointed at shoulders, hips, and knees. Incised on back of shoulder plate: "F 4/0 G". **(D)**

35-5 Gaultier Doll
**F. Gaultier
Paris, late 19th century
23"**

Bisque head, composition body and limbs; open mouth with four upper teeth, paperweight eyes, pierced ears, human hair wig; swivel neck, fully jointed; original clothing. Incised on back of head: "F.G." [within cartouche]. Body unmarked. [Although it is assumed that the "F.G." mark stands for F. Gaultier, documentary evidence is far from certain.] **(B)**

35-6 Eden Bébé
**Fleischmann & Blödel
Paris, c. 1895
22"**

Bisque head, composition body and limbs; open-closed mouth with row of upper teeth, brown glass eyes, pierced ears, human hair wig; swivel neck, fully jointed. Incised on back of head: "EDEN BEBE//PARIS//9//DEPOSE". [Although a German firm, Fleischmann & Blödel had a Parisian branch and became a founding member of S.F.B.J. in 1899.) **(B)**

35-7 Chérie
A. Lanternier & Cie.
Limoges, France, c. 1900
22"

Bisque head, composition body and limbs; open mouth with five upper teeth, glass eyes, pierced ears, human hair wig; swivel neck, fully jointed. Incised on back of head: [first two words within rectangle] "FABRICATION//FRANÇAIS //AL & Cie//LIMOGES//CHÉRIE 9". **(C)**

35-8 Jeanne D'Arc
Mlle. Marguerite de
**   Raphelis-Soissan**
Paris, 1920
14"

J. Verlingue bisque head, composition body and limbs; open-closed mouth with five upper teeth, glass pupil-less eyes, human hair wig; swivel neck, jointed at shoulders and hips. Incised on back of head "J V" [for J. Verlingue], separated by an anchor. Stamped on chest: "JEANNE// D'ARC//B.S.G.D.G." **(C)**

36 | Jumeau

The Jumeau establishment (Maison Jumeau), the recipient of many awards at the major 19th-century trade fairs, began manufacturing dolls when Pierre Francois Jumeau, in a partnership called Belton & Jumeau, established a doll factory in Paris in 1843. Although the death of Belton brought the partnership to an end, the dolls that Belton & Jumeau produced were among the great successes at London's Great Exhibition of 1851. The Germans took note of these dolls, remarking with some satisfaction that the dolls themselves were of no great merit, but that their clothing was exceptional and "in the latest style." Once Jumeau opened his own factory in Montreuil in 1873, Jumeau dolls were in demand for export because of their exquisite clothing. By this time, Jumeau heads were enjoying a reputation for fine painting and delicate shading, but Jumeau bodies were considered disappointingly crude. Emile Jumeau, Jumeau's eldest son, changed all this by establishing a factory that could handle all stages of production—from the kilns that fired the heads to the seamstresses who stitched the clothes. The result, once Jumeau was freed from importing parts, was the world-famous Jumeau facial expression, with its bewitching paperweight eyes. As one expert puts it, "a collector who has once seen and handled a Jumeau will always be able to recognize them again." By 1894 Emile Jumeau was called "Roi des Poupées"—the Doll King—and his dolls were in demand worldwide. But, in the face of growing German competition, the days of glory were swiftly numbered. In 1899, under intense economic pressure, Jumeau became a participating member of the S.F.B.J. syndicate (see section 37). Although the company's name survived, the quality of its dolls declined measurably. The dolls on the following pages attest to the splendor that was Jumeau; other Jumeaus are shown in sections 16, 20, and 21.

36-0 Bébé Jumeau (color plate, left)
Emile Jumeau
Paris, after 1878
20"

Bisque head, composition body and limbs; closed mouth, paperweight eyes, molded eyebrows, pierced ears, cork crown, human hair wig; swivel neck, fully jointed. Stamped on body: "JUMEAU//MEDAILLE D'OR//PARIS". [Redressed, using lace from original garments] **(B)**

Bébé Jumeau (color plate, center)
Emile Jumeau
Paris, after 1878
27"

Bisque head, composition body and limbs; closed mouth, paperweight eyes, pierced ears, cork crown, human hair wig; swivel neck, fully jointed; original clothing. Incised on back of head: "DÉPOSE//E 12 J" [with "8" and a check mark added in red ink]. **(B)**

Bébé Jumeau (color plate, right)
Emile Jumeau

Paris, after 1878
22"

Bisque head, composition body and limbs; closed mouth, paperweight eyes, molded eyebrows, pierced ears, cork crown, human hair wig; swivel neck, fully jointed. [Jumeau stamp on body obliterated during restoration.] **(B)**

36-2 Closed-Mouth Jumeau
Maison Jumeau
Paris, after 1878
15"

36-1 Emile Jumeau Doll
Maison Jumeau
Paris, after 1878
15"

Bisque head, composition body and limbs; closed mouth, paperweight eyes, pierced ears, cork crown, human hair wig; swivel neck, fully jointed. Incised on back of head: "DÉPOSÉ//TETE JUMEAU//B^{TE} SGDG//6". Stamped on body: "JUMEAU//MEDAILLE D'OR//PARIS". [This doll was once owned by Ethel Barrymore.] **(B)**

Bisque head, composition body and limbs; closed mouth, paperweight eyes, pierced ears, cork crown, human hair wig; swivel neck, fully jointed. Back of head incised: "DÉPOSÉ//TETE JUMEAU//B^{TE} SGDG//6". Body stamped: "JUMEAU/MEDAILLE D'OR//PARIS". **(B)**

36-4 "Long-Face" Jumeau
Maison Jumeau
Paris, after 1878
26"

Elongated bisque head, composition body and limbs; closed mouth, paperweight eyes, applied pierced ears, cork crown, human hair wig; swivel neck, fully jointed (except wrists); original clothing. Incised on head: "12". Stamped on body: "JUMEAU// MEDAILLE D'OR//PARIS". [The "long-face" Jumeau is sometimes called the "Cody" Jumeau, since tradition has it that William Cody ("Buffalo Bill") purchased such a doll on a European tour in 1887. There is some evidence that these long-faced heads may have been made for Jumeau by F. Simonne, Paris.) **(A)**

36-3 Closed-Mouth No. 1 Jumeau
Maison Jumeau
Paris, after 1878
9"

Bisque head, composition body and limbs; closed mouth, brown paperweight eyes, pierced ears, cork crown, human hair wig; swivel neck, fully jointed. Head unmarked [many Jumeau bébés were unmarked]. Stamped on body: "JUMEAU/MEDAILLE D'OR/ PARIS". **(B)**

36-5 Closed-Mouth Emile Jumeau Doll
Maison Jumeau
Paris, after 1878
24"

Bisque head, composition body and limbs; closed mouth, large

paperweight eyes, pierced ears, cork crown, human hair wig; swivel neck, fully jointed (except wrists), original clothing. Incised on back of head: "DÉPOSÉ//TETE JUMEAU//B^{TE} SGDG//11//[black check mark]/H4". Stamped on body: "JUMEAU//MEDAILLE D'OR//PARIS". **(B)**

36-6 Bébé Jumeau
Maison Jumeau
Paris, after 1889
26"

Bisque head, composition body and limbs; closed mouth, brown glass eyes, pierced ears, cork crown, human hair wig; swivel neck, fully jointed. Incised on back of head: "DÉPOSÉ//TETE JU-MEAU//B^{TE} SGDG//12". Stamped on body: BÉBÉ JUMEAU//Hors Con-cours 1889//DÉPOSÉ". **(B)**

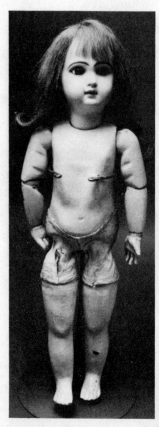

36-7 Bébé Marcheur (Walking Jumeau)
Emile Jumeau
Paris, 1895
22"

Bisque head, composition body and limbs; closed mouth, paperweight eyes, pierced ears, cork crown, human hair wig; swivel neck, fully jointed; legs attach to steel mechanism [disguised by kid drawers] that enables doll to walk. Incised on back of head: "DÉPOSÉ //TETE JUMEAU//B^{TE} S.G.D.G.//9// [black check mark]." Body unmarked. **(B)**

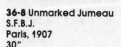

36-8 Unmarked Jumeau
S.F.B.J.
Paris, 1907
30"

Bisque head, composition body and limbs; open mouth with row of upper teeth, paperweight eyes, pierced ears, human hair wig; swivel neck, fully jointed; original clothing. Incised on back of head: "1907//15". Body unmarked. [The Jumeau name was carried on by the S.F.B.J. after 1899.] **(B)**

37 | S.F.B.J. and Unis France

Once the Germans began to imitate French bébés, and produced them in quantity and at low prices, the destiny of French doll manufacturers was sealed. Unable to compete successfully, most of the surviving French firms signed an agreement on March 29, 1899 to form a syndicate known as the Société Française de Fabrication de Bébés et Jouets, better known to collectors as S.F.B.J. These firms originally included Jumeau, Bru, Fleischmann et Blödel, Rabery et Delphieu, and Pintel et Godchaux. A few years later P.H. Schmitz and Ad. Bouchet were added with Daniel et Cie joining in 1911. Although the syndicate freely used German parts (including Simon & Halbig heads), it is a mistake to assume that S.F.B.J. dolls are "German" dolls. The syndicate continued to make heads in French factories, boasting in 1911 that they were making 5 million dolls a year. With 7 million dolls in production in 1921, the year the Unis France mark was introduced, it is no wonder why S.F.B.J. dolls are among the most common French dolls found by collectors. These dolls vary in quality from the excellence of S.F.B.J. Jumeaus to perfectly wretched dolls with almost featureless faces. Among the most prized S.F.B.J. dolls are French character dolls, those with fixed glass eyes being particularly attractive. Although firms such as Bru and Jumeau were absorbed by the syndicate, the dolls made by these member firms continued to be manufactured, so that as late as 1921 Bébé Bru, Eden Bébé, and Bébé Jumeau were still being marketed under their old names.

37-0 Bisque-Head Doll (color plate)
S.F.B.J.
Paris, after 1899
22"

Bisque head, composition body and limbs; open mouth with row of upper teeth, paperweight eyes, pierced ears, human hair wig; swivel neck, fully jointed; original clothing. Incised on back of head: "R//S.F.B.J.//PARIS//10". **(C)**

37-1 Bisque-Head Doll
S.F.B.J.
Paris, after 1899
23"

Bisque head, composition body and limbs; open mouth with six upper teeth, brown glass eyes, molded eyebrows, pierced ears, human hair wig; swivel neck, fully jointed; original clothing. Incised on back of head: " +//S.F.B.J.//301/PARIS". **(B)**

37-2 Character Doll ("Twerp")
S.F.B.J.
Paris, early 20th century
18"

Bisque head on composition toddler body, curled toes; open-
closed mouth with two upper
teeth, glass sleeping eyes, human
hair wig; swivel head, fully jointed.
Incised on back of head: "23//
FRANCE//247//PARIS". [This doll is
known to collectors as "Twerp."]
(B)

37-3 Character Baby ("Laughing
    Jumeau")
S.F.B.J.
Paris, after 1909
9" (seated)

Bisque head on composition bent-
limb baby body; open-closed
mouth, two upper teeth, glass
sleeping eyes; swivel neck,
jointed at shoulders and hips. Incised on back of head: "S.F.B.J.//
236//PARIS". **(C)**

37-4 French Soldier and Nurse

S.F.B.J.
Paris, c. 1918
5" (each)

Bisque head, composition body and limbs; closed mouth (soldier), open mouth with teeth (nurse), glass eyes (with no white showing); swivel neck, jointed at shoulders and hips. Incised on back of head: "S.F.B.J.//301//PARIS". [Photographed with toy French ambulance of the period.] **(Each, E)**

37-5 Unis France Doll
S.F.B.J.
Paris, c. 1922
11"

Bisque head, composition body and limbs; open-closed mouth with two upper teeth, sleeping eyes with lashes, human hair wig; swivel neck, fully jointed. Incised on back of head: [within oval] "UNIS// FRANCE"; [to left of oval] "11"; [to right of oval] "149"; [beneath oval] "251". **(D)**

38 | Heubach and Other Famous German Doll Makers

The worldwide success of French bisque dolls was the envy of the young enterprising manufacturers in Thuringia who promptly followed one of the eternal economic verities: imitation. Consequently, these German entrepreneurs copied French bébés and marketed them more effectively, selling them more cheaply than their French competitors. So successful were the Germans, in fact, that by the end of the 19th century German bisque dolls dominated the world market. Waltershausen, Ohrdruf, Köppelsdorf, and Ilmenau were among the porcelain manufacturing centers that made dolls and dolls' heads, but Sonneberg was the chief center of German production. Illustrated in the following pages are dolls by Gebrüder Heubach, Ernst Heubach, Heinrich Handwerck, C.F. Kling, Franz Schmidt, Adolf Wislizenus, Kley & Hahn, Schoenau & Hoffmeister, and several other German doll makers. Dolls by Kämmer & Reinhardt, Simon & Halbig, J.D. Kestner, and Armand Marseille are illustrated in the sections that follow.

38-0 Character Boy (color plate)
Gebrüder Heubach
Lichte, Thür., c. 1910
18"

Bisque head, composition body and limbs; open mouth with two lower teeth, intaglio eyes, molded and painted blonde hair; swivel neck, fully jointed. Incised on back of head: "[lower-case "H" with long tail at end of letter]//Germany". **(D)**

38-1 Twin Character Dolls
Gebrüder Heubach
Lichte, Thür., early 20th century
15" (each)

Bisque head, composition body and limbs; open mouth with four upper teeth, one doll with brown glass eyes, the other with blue glass sleeping eyes, human hair wig; swivel neck, fully jointed; dolls redressed as twins. Incised on back of heads: "8192//Germany//Gebrüder Heubach//[potter's mark of half-sunflower over bottom half of circle with intertwined "GH" over "DEP" within oblong shape]//G 1 H". **(Each E)**

38-2 Smiling Girl (with Figurine)
Gebrüder Heubach
Lichte, Thür., c. 1920
11½"

Bisque head, composition body and limbs; open-closed mouth with row of upper teeth, intaglio eyes, molded and painted blonde hair with turquoise glazed hair ribbon; swivel neck, fully jointed. Incised on back of head: "77 HEU/BACH [within square] 63//Germany". "80" stamped in green before mark. [Photographed with 7½" Heubach figurine.] **[Girl, D; figurine, E)**

38-3 Twins
Ernst Heubach
Köppelsdorf, Thür., early 20th century
22" (each)

Bisque head, composition body and limbs; open mouth with four upper teeth, glass sleeping eyes with lashes, human hair wig; swivel neck, fully jointed. Incised on back of girl's head: "Heubach-Köppelsdorf//

250-1//Germany". Mark on boy is identical, except for number, "250-3". **(Each, D)**

**38-4 German Bisque Doll
Heinrich Handwerck
Gotha, Thür., early 20th century
36"**

Bisque head, composition body and limbs; open mouth with four upper teeth, brown glass sleeping eyes, pierced ears, human hair wig; swivel neck, fully jointed. Incised on back of head: "16½//Germany//HANDWERCK//7½". **(C)**

**38-5 Bébé Cosmopolite
Heinrich Handwerck
Gotha, Thür., 1895-1902
24"**

Simon & Halbig bisque head, composition body and limbs; open mouth with four upper teeth, brown glass sleeping eyes, human hair wig; swivel neck, fully jointed. Incised on back of head: "Germany//HEINRICH HANDWERCK//SIMON & HALBIG". Stamped on right thigh: HEINRICH HANDWERCK //Germany". Label on original box (not photographed) includes Handwerck eight-pointed star trademark and "GENUINE HANDWERCK DOLL//HANDWERCK'S//BÉBÉ COSMOPOLITE". [This doll was given as a premium for selling Burnett's Standard Flavoring Extracts and is photographed with an original Burnett bottle.] **(C)**

38-6 German Bisque Shoulder-Head Doll (left)
Heinrich Handwerck
Gotha, Thür., c. 1900
18" (entire doll), 4" (shoulder head)

Bisque shoulder head on kid body with bisque forearms; open mouth with four upper teeth, glass eyes, human hair wig; jointed at shoulders, hips, and knees. Incised on back of shoulder plate: "MADE IN GERMANY [around a horseshoe-shaped mark]//1900-4/0". **(D)**

German Bisque-Head Doll (right)
Charles M. Bergmann
Waltershausen, Thür., early 20th century
22"

Bisque head, composition body and limbs; open mouth with four upper teeth, glass sleeping eyes with lashes, human hair wig; swivel neck, fully jointed. Incised on back of head: "287//C.M. Bergmann [in script]//BB1//Germany". **(D)**

38-7 Bisque Shoulder Head
C.F. Kling & Co.
Ohrdruf, Thür., late 19th century
21" (entire doll), 5½" (shoulder head)

Bisque shoulder head, cloth body with kid forearms and feet; closed mouth, brown glass eyes, molded and painted blonde hair; jointed at shoulders, hips, and knees; original clothing. Incised on back of shoul-

der plate: "266 [bell with 'K' at center] 8". **(C)**

38-8 Twin "Breathers"
Franz Schmidt & Co.
Georgenthal, Thür., after 1902
7½"

Bisque head, composition toddler-type body and limbs; open mouth with two teeth, glass sleeping eyes, human hair wig, pierced nostrils, swivel neck, jointed at shoulders and hips. Incised on back of head: "1295//FS&C.//Made in [script]//Germany [script]". [Dolls with open pierced nostrils are sometimes called "breathers" by collectors.] **(Each, E)**

38-9 Bisque-Head Doll
Adolf Wislizenus
Waltershausen, Thür., early 20th century
28"

Bisque head, composition body and limbs; open mouth with four upper teeth, brown glass sleeping eyes, molded eyebrows, pierced
ears, human hair wig; swivel neck, fully jointed. Incised on back of
head: ``A W//W''. **(D)**

38-10 Walküre
Kley & Hahn
Ohrdruf, Thür., after 1902
28"

Bisque head, composition body and limbs; open mouth, brown glass eyes, molded eyebrows, pierced ears, human hair wig; swivel neck, fully jointed. Incised on back of head: "16//Walkure//Germany//14½". **(D)**

38-11 Bisque-Head Doll
Schoenau & Hoffmeister
Burggrub, Bavaria, after 1901
23"

Bisque head, composition body and limbs; open mouth with four upper teeth, brown glass eyes, human hair wig; swivel neck, fully jointed. Incised on back of head: "S H [on either side of a five-pointed star containing the initials "P B".] ["SH" stands for "Porzellan-fabrik Burggrub" or "Porcelain Factory of Burggrub."] **(D)**

38-12 Character Boy
Alt, Beck & Gottschalck
Nauendorf, Thür., after 1909
15"

Bisque head on composition bent-limb baby body; open mouth with two upper teeth and tongue, brown glass sleeping eyes with lashes, molded and painted hair; swivel neck, jointed at shoulders and hips; redressed. Incised on back of head: "40/13 ABG [inter-twined] 57". **(D)**

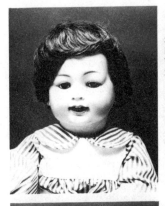

**38-13 Character Baby
König & Wernicke
Waltershausen, Thür., after 1912
24"**

Bisque head, composition body and limbs; open mouth with two upper teeth and tremble tongue, brown sleeping eyes, human hair wig; swivel neck, fully jointed. Incised on back of head: "K & W//170//13". **(C)**

**38-14 "Kidbody" Doll in Original Box
Cuno & Otto Dressel
Sonneberg, Thür., early 20th century
18" (entire doll)
5" (shoulder head)**

Bisque shoulder head on kid body with bisque forearms; open mouth with six upper teeth, glass sleeping eyes, human hair wig; jointed at shoulders and knees. Incised on back of head: "Germany//[winged helmet trademark within circle]". Label on box: "KIDBODY DOLLS//Made in [winged helmet trademark] Germany". Doll and box are numbered "5406FB45". **(E)**

38-15 French Gendarme
Steiff
Giengen, Würtemberg, c. 1920
15"

Felt doll with painted moustache, real hair under cap, button eyes, seam down middle of face. Metal button in one ear is Steiff identification mark ("Knopf im Ohr," "Bouton dans L'oreille," etc.) Extra-large feet, another Steiff feature, enables doll to stand. [Doll bears a striking resemblance to Charles de Gaulle.] **(C)**

39 | Kämmer & Reinhardt

This famous partnership, with Kämmer serving as the modeler and Reinhardt handling the business affairs, came into being in 1886 and established its lasting fame by introducing its famous line of character dolls (a term invented by K & R), of which "Baby"(39-2) is perhaps the best known. (Collectors once believed that this doll was modeled on the son of the Kaiser, and called it "Kaiser Baby" or "Prince Otto," but it was actually based on the son of the sculptor who created it.) The K & R character dolls were a great success and are eagerly sought by collectors today, especially those with sulky expressions called "pouties." Most K & R dolls feature Simon & Halbig heads, but it is a mistake to think of these as S & H dolls since they were made to exact specifications from the K & H models. (Many collectors continue to think that K & R dolls are actually S & H dolls because the K & R portion of the double mark is often obscured by the wig). Kämmer & Reinhardt was an innovative company that not only pioneered in the development of unusual eye mechanisms but also effected changes in doll anatomy to accommodate changing fashions in clothes. When little girls' dresses became quite short in the 1920s, and exposed ball-jointed knees appeared ugly in consequence, K & R was shrewd enough to introduce a doll with long lower legs that allowed the joint to occur above the knee. (Despite the fact that collectors persist in believing that these dolls have "teenage bodies," the dolls were intended to be little girls.)

39-0 Bisque-Head Doll (color plate)
Kämmer & Reinhardt
Waltershausen, Thür., after 1909
30"

Bisque head, composition body and limbs; open mouth with four upper teeth, brown glass sleeping eyes with lashes, pierced ears, replacement wig; swivel neck, fully jointed. Incised on back of head: "K & R" [the ampersand falls within a six-pointed star]. **(C)**

39-1 K & R Miniature
Kämmer & Reinhardt
Waltershausen, Thür., after 1895
6"

All-bisque doll with molded shoes and stockings; open mouth with two upper teeth, glass sleeping eyes, human hair wig; swivel neck, jointed at shoulders and hips; original clothing. Incised on back of head: "K [ampersand within six-pointed star] R". **(E)**

39-2 "Baby" (Mold #100)
Kämmer & Reinhardt
Waltershausen, Thür., 1909
15"

Bisque head, composition bent-limb body; open-closed mouth, intaglio eyes, molded and painted hair; swivel neck, jointed at shoulders and hips. Incised on back of head: "36//K [ampersand within six-pointed star] R//100". ["Baby" was very likely the first bent-limb baby doll; mold #100 was among K & R's earliest character dolls. Collectors occasionally call this famous doll "Kaiser Baby" or "Prince Otto."] **(D)**

39-3 Mold #76
Kämmer & Reinhardt
Waltershausen, Thür., after 1905
28"

Simon & Halbig bisque head, composition body and limbs; open mouth with three upper teeth, sleeping eyes with lashes, molded eyebrows, pierced ears, human hair wig; swivel neck, fully jointed. Incised on back of head: "K [ampersand within six-pointed star] R//SIMON & HALBIG//76". **(D)**

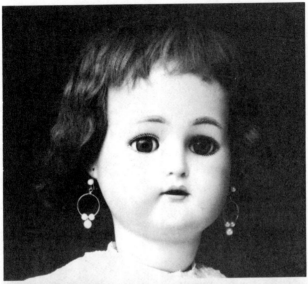

39-4 Mold #117
Kämmer & Reinhardt
Waltershausen, Thür., after 1905
26"

Simon & Halbig bisque head, composition body and limbs; closed mouth, brown glass eyes, human hair wig; swivel neck, fully jointed. Incised on back of head: "K [ampersand within six-pointed star] R// SIMON & HALBIG//117". **(B)**

**39-5 Character Baby
Kämmer & Reinhardt
Waltershausen, Thür., after 1905
23" (seated)**

Simon & Halbig head on composition bent-limb baby body; open mouth with two upper teeth, glass eyes, human hair wig; swivel neck, jointed at shoulders and hips. Incised on back of head: "K [ampersand within six-pointed star] R// SIMON & HALBIG//128". **(B)**

**39-6 Bisque-Head Doll
Kämmer & Reinhardt
Waltershausen, Thür., early 20th
  century
23"**

Simon & Halbig bisque head on composition body with composition limbs; open mouth with two upper teeth, glass sleeping eyes with lashes, pierced ears, human hair wig; swivel neck, fully jointed, redressed. Incised on back of head: "HALBIG//K [ampersand within six-pointed star] R//11". **(D)**

40 | Simon & Halbig

Next to Armand Marseille, the firm of Simon & Halbig was the second largest maker of dolls' heads in Germany. The company originated in 1869 in Gräfenhain, Thuringia, for the production of porcelain, but, since one of its founders, Wilhelm Simon, was also a toy manufacturer who produced dolls, the new firm decided to take advantage of the growing vogue for bisque-headed dolls by producing their own dolls' heads, both for their own use and for other companies as well. For this reason, S & H shoulder heads are among the earliest marked bisques available to collectors, although precise dating is difficult. (The famous "S & H" mark first used the ampersand in 1905; "SH" marks without the ampersand consequently date before 1905.) Simon & Halbig produced high-quality bisque heads that were much in demand by French manufacturers, including Jumeau. That the company's heads were also frequently used on the most expensive mechanical dolls made by Roullet and Decamps and on the earliest Edison phonograph dolls attests to their fineness. The company rarely made character heads for its own use, but did produce them in large numbers for Kämmer & Reinhardt, a dependence that no doubt led to K & R's acquisition of the S & H firm in 1916. Mass-produced dolls by S & H and Armand Marseille brought bisque dolls within reach of most children, a situation that resulted in some very poorly molded heads. Unlike Armand Marseille heads, however, those by Simon & Halbig are generally of good to excellent quality.

40-O Santa Doll (color plate)
Simon & Halbig (head)
Gräfenhain, Thür., after 1905
35"

Bisque head, composition body and limbs; open mouth with four upper teeth, glass sleeping eyes, pierced ears, human hair wig; swivel neck, fully jointed, original clothing. Incised on back of head: "S & H 1849//'DEP'//Germany//SANTA//16". [Between 1900 and 1910 Simon & Halbig produced bisque heads for Hamburger & Co. of Berlin, Nürnberg, and New York, manufacturers of the Santa doll.] **(C)**

40-1 Simon & Halbig Mold #1079
Simon & Halbig
Gräfenhain, Thür., before 1905
28"

Bisque head, composition body
and limbs; open mouth with four
upper teeth, brown glass sleeping
eyes, pierced ears, human hair
wig; swivel neck, fully jointed. Incised on back of head: "SH 1079
DEP//14". **(C)**

40-2 Simon & Halbig Mold #1079
Simon & Halbig
Gräfenhain, Thür., before 1905
24"

Bisque head, composition body
and limbs; open mouth with four
upper teeth, brown glass sleeping
eyes, pierced ears, mohair wig;
swivel neck, fully jointed, original
clothing. Incised on back of head:
"SH 1079-12//DEP". [Identical, except in size to 40-1; a good example of how choice of wig and
costume can change "personality."] **(D)**

40-3 Simon & Halbig Mold #1019
Simon & Halbig
Gräfenhain, Thür. , after 1905
23"

Bisque head, composition body
and limbs; open mouth with four
upper teeth, glass sleeping eyes,
pierced ears, human hair wig;
swivel neck, fully jointed. Incised
on back of head: "S. & H. 1019//
DEP//Germany//12". **(D)**

40-4 Bisque-Head Doll
Charles M. Bergmann
Waltershausen, Thür., after 1910
28"

Simon & Halbig bisque head, composition body and limbs; open mouth with four upper teeth, glass sleeping eyes with lashes, molded eyebrows, pierced ears, human hair wig; swivel neck, fully jointed. Incised on back of head: "C.M. BERGMANN//SIMON & HAL-BIG//14". **(D)**

40-5 Simon & Halbig Doll for
    Gimbels Bros.
Simon & Halbig
Gräfenhain, Thür., after 1905
22"

Simon & Halbig bisque head, composition body and limbs; open mouth with four upper teeth; glass sleeping eyes, human hair wig; swivel neck, fully jointed. Incised on back of head: "Germany //SIMON & HALBIG". Stamped in red on body: "[within rectangle] Gimbel Bros.//Germany". [Made for the famous American department store, with branches in New York and Philadelphia.] **(D)**

40-6 Simon & Halbig Miniatures with Rococo-style Wigs
Simon & Halbig
Gräfenhain, Thür., after 1905 to c. 1916
Left: 6" (entire doll), 1¼" (shoulder head)
Center: 8" (entire doll), 2½" (shoulder head)
Right: 6" (entire doll), 1¼" (shoulder head)

Bisque-shoulder heads on cloth bodies with bisque forearms and legs with molded shoes; closed mouths, glass eyes, human hair wigs; jointed at shoulders and hips. Incised on back of shoulder plates: "S & H// 1160". **(Each, E)**

41 | J. D. Kestner

By the middle of the 19th century, the Kestner family, long established as one of Germany's most prolific doll makers, was creating dolls in both papier-mâché and wood, while glazed china heads were made after 1860. Although the family eventually produced dolls of every material, including wax and celluloid, the bisque heads, bearing the unique Kestner marks, are the most familiar to collectors. Kestner doll-faced heads are often somewhat chubby and dimpled, appearing "too Germanic" to some and charming to others, but there is no disputing that the firm's oriental dolls (32-0), character babies (41-7), and lady dolls (19-0) are collectors' favorites today. Given its contemporary reputation for quality, Kestner was the first firm chosen by George Borgfeldt to manufacture Rose O'Neill's Kewpies. Kestner heads are not always marked "JDK", but are frequently marked "Germany" together with the numbers denoting the head size. This is the so-called "Kestner Alphabet," which is decoded and described in full in the Colemans' indispensable **Collector's Encyclopedia of Dolls.**

41-0 Hilda (color plate)
J.D. Kestner, Jr.
Waltershausen, Thür., 1914
13"

Bisque head on composition bent-limb baby body; open mouth with two upper teeth, glass sleeping eyes, molded and painted hair; swivel neck, jointed at hips and shoulders. Incised on back of head: "Hilda// J.D.K. Jr. 191//Gesgesch N. 1070//made in//Germany". **(C)**

41-1 Kestner Mold #146
J.D. Kestner, Jr.
Waltershausen, Thür.
c. 1892-1910
26"

Bisque head, composition body and limbs; open mouth with four upper teeth; brown glass sleeping eyes with lashes, mohair wig; swivel neck, fully jointed. Incised on back of head: "Made in//M Germany 16//146". Plaster pate numbered: "146//16". **(D)**

41-2 Mold #164
J.D. Kestner, Jr.
Waltershausen, Thür,. 1892-1910
34"

Bisque head, composition body and limbs; open mouth with four upper teeth, brown glass sleeping eyes, molded eyebrows, human hair wig; swivel neck, fully jointed. Incised on back of head: "Made in//M¼ Germany 16½//164". **(D)**

41-3 Mold #167
J.D. Kestner, Jr.
Waltershausen, Thür., 1892-1910
22"

Bisque head, composition body and limbs; open mouth with four upper teeth, glass sleeping eyes, molded eyebrows, human hair wig; swivel neck, fully jointed. Incised on back of head: "H½ Made in 12½//Germany". **(D)**

41-4 Mold #171
J.D. Kestner, Jr.
Waltershausen, Thür., after 1910
32"

Bisque head, composition body and limbs; open mouth with four upper teeth, brown glass sleeping eyes with lashes, human hair wig; swivel neck, fully jointed. Incised on back of head: "Made in [in script]//N½ Germany [in script] 17½//171". Plaster pate numbered: "171//17½". **(C)**

41-5 Rare 10" Kestner Doll
J.D. Kestner, Jr.
Waltershausen, Thür., c. 1914
10"

Bisque head, composition body and limbs; open mouth with two upper teeth, brown glass sleeping eyes, human hair wig; swivel neck, fully jointed. Incised on back of head: "Made in//[illegible] Germany 3//143". **(E)**

41-6 Mold #250
J.D. Kestner, Jr.
Waltershausen, Thür., early 20th century
42"

Bisque head, composition body and limbs; open mouth with four upper teeth, sleeping glass eyes with lashes, pierced ears, replacement wig; swivel neck, fully jointed. Incised on back of head: "Made in//Germany//J.D.K.//250//Germany//100". **(B)**

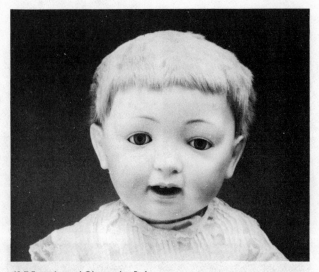

41-7 Fur-wigged Character Baby
J.D. Kestner, Jr.
Waltershausen, Thür., after 1909
23"

Bisque head on composition bent-limb baby body; open mouth with
two lower teeth, glass sleeping eyes, fur wig; swivel neck, jointed at
shoulders and hips. Wig obscures mark. **(D)**

42 | Armand Marseille

Armand Marseille was the most prolific of the German doll makers
and manufactured a wide range of cheap bisque heads. Like Simon
& Halbig, the company produced heads for other firms, including
Charles Bergmann, George Borgfeldt, and Louis Wolf, and its output
varies widely in quality from very badly-made bisque heads to beautiful dolls that compare favorably with those of almost any other German manufacturer. Until recent discoveries by German historians
Jürgen and Marianne Cieslik, Armand Marseille was something of a
man of mystery. Some writers believed him to have been born in
France or in Riga, and some believed him to have been related to
Ernst Heubach of Köppelsdorf (both were partners in the United Köppelsdorf Porcelain Factory). In fact, however, Marseille "was the son of
a Huguenot architect, born in 1856 in St. Petersburg, Russia. As a
young man he traveled throughout Europe and eventually settled

near Sonneberg, bought a toy factory in 1884 and a porcelain factory in 1885 and started to produce porcelain jugs and pipe heads." Marseille made his first bisque heads in 1890, and the rest is history. Because of the very large number of Armand Marseille dolls produced, dolls marked "AM" appear in many different sections of this book; consult the index of makers under "Marseille" for their exact locations.

42-O Mold #370 (color plate)
Armand Marseille
Köppelsdorf, Thür., c. 1904
26" (entire doll), 7" (shoulder head)

Bisque shoulder head on cloth body with cloth limbs; open mouth with four upper teeth, brown glass sleeping eyes, molded eyebrows, human hair wig; jointed at shoulders, elbows, hips, and knees; original clothing. Incised on back of shoulder plate: "370//AM 8 DEP//Made in Germany". [One of the most frequently produced Armand Marseilles dolls.] **(E)**

42-1 Mold #370
Armand Marseille
Köppelsdorf, Thür., c. 1904
23" (entire doll)
7" (shoulder head)

Bisque shoulder head, kid body with composition arms; open mouth with four upper teeth, brown glass sleeping eyes with lashes, human hair wig and human hair eyebrows; fully jointed body. Incised on back of head: "370//AM-7-DEP//Armand Marseille". [This doll, the preceding doll, and the following two dolls are all different sizes of the same mold. They form a dramatic study of how choice of costume and wig affect the "personality" of a doll.] **(E)**

42-2 Nun
Armand Marseille
Köppelsdorf, Thür., c. 1904
20" (entire doll)
5½" (shoulder head)

Bisque shoulder head on cloth body with bisque forearms; open mouth with four upper teeth, brown glass eyes; jointed at shoulders and hips. Incised on back of head: "370//AM-[illegible]-DEP/Armand Marseille". [When found this doll wore the remnants of a nun's habit; it was redressed in the Dominican habit by a contemporary nun.] **(E)**

42-3 Bisque Shoulder Head Doll
Armand Marseille
Köppelsdorf, Thür., c. 1904
19" (entire doll)
5" (shoulder head)

Bisque shoulder head on kid body with bisque forearms; open mouth with four upper teeth, glass sleeping eyes, human hair wig; jointed at shoulders, hips, and knees; original clothing. Incised on back of shoulder plate: "370//A.M. 5/0x DEP". **(E)**

42-4 Just Me
Armand Marseille
Köppelsdorf, Thür., early 20th
  century
9"

Bisque head, composition limbs
and body; closed mouth, glass
sleeping eyes, human hair wig;
swivel neck, jointed at shoulders
and hips. Incised on back of
head: "Just ME//Registered//Germany//A. 310/ 7/0. M". ["Just Me"
was distributed by George Borgfeldt.] **(D)**

42-5 Small Bisque-Head Doll (left)
Armand Marseille

Köppelsdorf, Thür., c. 1925
8"

Bisque head, composition body and limbs; open mouth with four upper teeth, glass sleeping eyes, human hair wig; swivel neck, jointed at
shoulders and hips; original clothing. Incised on back of head: "Ger-
many//A 12/0 M". **(F)**

Bisque Shoulder Head (right)
Armand Marseille
Köppelsdorf, Thür., c. 1904
4½"

Open mouth with four upper teeth, brown glass sleeping eyes, human
hair wig. Incised on back of head: "A 1776 M//C.O.D. 4/0 DEP//Made in
Germany". Label on front of breast plate: "[in ink] 114 B 4/0". [May be a
sales sample. Head was made by Armand Marseille for Cuno & Otto
Dressel, Sonneberg, Germany, the "C.O.D." of the label.] **(F)**

43 | Käthe Kruse

When Käthe Kruse's early dolls were first shown in America in 1911,
they were hailed as "art dolls with a capital A," a judgment that time
has not dimmed. Throughout her life, Käthe Kruse, the wife of a Berlin
sculptor, campaigned against rubber dolls, which she found
hideous, and bisque dolls, which she considered cold. What she
wanted was a soft doll, as realistic as possible, that would exercise the
"natural maternal instincts" of little girls. Instead, she created minor
works of art that are particularly appealing to adults. Käthe Kruse
dolls were at first based on Italian Renaissance sculptures of
children's heads; later, live models were used, including her own
children. Her dolls' faces were realistic to a high degree and are not
to be confused with character dolls that appear, by comparison,
almost as caricatures. The bodies of her baby dolls were weighted
with sand to create the feeling of holding a real baby. Most Käthe
Kruse dolls made before World War II have several features in common: they are durable, washable, soft, and supple, and are made by
hand, the latter quality one of the reasons for their high price. They
generally have the Käthe Kruse mark and serial number on the sole of
their left foot.

43-O Character Boy (color plate)
Käthe Kruse
German, c. 1925-30
15"

Fixative over cloth head on cloth body; painted and molded features, painted hair; jointed at shoulders and hips; original clothing. Signature in ink on bottom of left foot: "Käthe Kruse [in script]//S*6D". Stamped on bottom of right foot: "GERMANY". **(D)**

43-1 Emily
Käthe Kruse
German, c. 1948
14½"

Composition head on cloth body; painted and molded features, painted hair; jointed at shoulders and hips; original clothing. Stamped on left foot: "Käthe Kruse [in script]//61772". Stamped on right foot: "Made in Germany//US-Zone". On label: "Käthe Kruse [in script]//EMILY// x/9 //Original gekleidet". On second label: "Art Dolls Unique//[around circle] Käthe// Germany//Kruse//Germany". **(D)**

43-2 Modern Käthe Kruse Dolls
German, c. 1965
9½" (left), 10½" (right)

Composition heads, cloth bodies, painted features, synthetic hair wigs; unjointed. On labels: "ORIGINAL//Käthe Kruse [in script]//MODELL //HANNE KRUSE//Made in Germany". [Although modern Käthe Kruse

dolls are already collectors' items, they are in every way less satisfactory than early Käthe Kruses.] **(E)**

44 | Ludwig Greiner

The first patented dolls' heads in America were made of papier-mâché by Ludwig Greiner, who had emigrated from Germany to Philadelphia specifically to set up as a doll maker. Since most American dolls in the middle of the 19th century were made of wood or rag, with imported dolls relatively expensive, Greiner correctly saw a domestic market ripe for the skills he imported from his native country. Accordingly, he patented an improved papier-mâché head in 1858, although it is believed that his dolls were first produced several years before that date, all molded of equal quantities of paper, whiting, and rye flour, mixed with glue and strengthened at weak points with linen cloth. Early Greiners have black hair, parted down the middle in the manner of German china dolls of the same period. Those most eagerly sought by collectors are mounted on bodies by Jacob Lacmann. Many Greiner heads were lightly finished with varnish before sale, and this protective finish has badly discolored over the years. Greiner's patent was extended in 1872, and a greater variety of heads was made after this date, including a larger number of boy dolls and blondes.

44-O Blonde Greiner Doll (color plate)
Ludwig Greiner
Philadelphia, Pennsylvania, 1858-72
30"

Cloth-reinforced papier-mâché shoulder head, cloth body with leather arms; molded and painted features and blonde hair, turquoise eyes; jointed at shoulders, hips, and knees. Label on breast plate: "GREINER'S//PATENT HEADS//No 10//Pat. March 30TH '58". **(D)**

44-1 Greiner Doll
Ludwig Greiner
Philadelphia, Pennsylvania
1858-72
28"

Cloth-reinforced papier-mâché shoulder head, cloth body with kid arms; molded and painted features and hair; jointed at shoulders, hips, and knees. Label on back of shoulder plate: "GREINER'S//PATENT HEADS//Pat. Mar 30th, '58". **(D)**

44-2 Greiner Doll

Ludwig Greiner
Philadelphia, Pennsylvania, 1858-72
24" (entire doll), 7" (shoulder head)

Cloth-reinforced papier-mâché shoulder head, cloth body with wooden lower legs; molded and painted features and hair; turquoise eyes; jointed at shoulders, hips, and knees. Label on back of breast plate: "GREINER'S//PATENT HEADS//No. 8//Pat. Mar 30th, '58". **(D)**

44-3 Greiner Doll
Ludwig Greiner
Philadelphia, Pennsylvania
after 1872
17½" (entire doll)
5" (shoulder head)

Cloth-reinforced papier-mâché shoulder head on cloth body; molded and painted features and hair; jointed at shoulders, hips, and knees. Label on back of breast plate: "GREINER'S//PATENT DOLL HEADS//No. 5//Pat. Mar 30, '58. Ext. '72//Factory, 41 N. 4th [label torn]". **(D)**

45 | Fulper Pottery Co.

The cut-off of German imports during World War I led to many American attempts to simulate German bisque dolls, including heads made of flour in California (insects devoured the dolls) and the first bisque dolls made in America—by the Bisc Manufacturing Company of East Liverpool, Ohio (1917). The most successful American bisque dolls, however, were those made by the Fulper Pottery Co. of Flemington, New Jersey, between the years 1918 and 1920. These dolls are said to have featured heads made from molds obtained from Armand Marseille and were produced by Fulper at the encouragement of the Horsman Company, for whom many of the heads were made. Among the Fulper output were some all-bisque dolls, including Kewpies and the Peterkin doll (45-4) designed by Helen Trowbridge. The general appearance of Fulper dolls suggests an imitation of German dolls, though of poorer quality, although this hardly deters collecting, given the short period of their manufacture. The dolls with molded hair and intaglio eyes, in particular, are reminiscent of heads made by Gebrüder Heubach. By the time the company ceased doll production in 1920, Fulper was marketing ten girl models with swivel heads and eight baby models, all of them avidly sought by collectors today.

45-O Bisque-Head Boy (color plate, left)
Fulper Pottery Co.
Flemington, New Jersey, c. 1919
23"

Bisque head, composition body and limbs; open mouth, two upper teeth, glass sleeping eyes, human hair wig; swivel neck, fully jointed. Incised on back of head: "CMU [within triangle]//FULPER [within vertical rectangle]//Made in [in script]//USA [in script]//11". **(C)**

Bisque-Head Girl (color plate, right)
Fulper Pottery Co.
Flemington, New Jersey, c. 1919
21"

Bisque head, composition body and limbs; open mouth, two upper teeth, glass eyes, human hair wig; swivel neck, fully jointed. Same mark as boy, except that "Made in U.S.A." is in upper-case letters and number is "11-C". **(C)**

45-1 Two Fulper Dolls
Fulper Pottery Co.
Flemington, New Jersey, after 1918
Left: 17½" (entire doll), 5" (shoulder head)
Right: 15"

Left: Bisque shoulder head on cloth body with bisque forearms; open mouth with two upper teeth, glass sleeping eyes, human hair wig; jointed at shoulders, hips, and knees. Incised on back of head: "CMU" [in triangle] over "FULPER" [in vertical rectangle]//SS-8½". **(D)**

Right: Bisque head, composition body with painted shoes and stockings; open mouth with two upper teeth, glass eyes, human hair wig; swivel neck, jointed at shoulders and hips. Incised on back of head: [Same Fulper mark, but with "Made in USA" in script and no number.] **(D)**

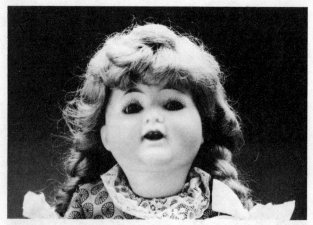

45-2 Fulper Colonial Doll
Colonial Toy Manufacturing Co.
New York City, after 1918
18"

Fulper Pottery Co. bisque head, composition body and limbs; open mouth with two upper teeth and tongue, glass sleeping eyes, human hair wig; swivel neck, fully-jointed. Incised on back of head: "[Fulper mark as in 45-0]//COLONIAL//DOLL//MADE IN//U.S.A.//A 15 C". **(D)**

45-3 Fulper-Horsman Baby Doll
E.I. Horsman & Aetna Doll Co.
New York City, c. 1920
14" (seated)

Fulper Pottery Co. bisque head on composition bent-limb baby body; open mouth with two upper teeth, glass eyes, human hair wig; jointed at shoulders and hips. Incised on back of head: "[within vertical rectangle] FULPER//[within circle pierced by rectangle] "Made in USA//HORSMAN//DOLL// H [illegible numerals]". **(D)**

45-4 All-Bisque Peterkin
Fulper Pottery Co.
Flemington, New Jersey, c. 1919
11"

All-bisque doll, jointed at shoulders; closed mouth, intaglio flirting eyes, molded and painted hair. [This doll, designed by Helen Trowbridge, is based on the famed title character of Howard Pyle's story "Peterkin and the Little Grey Hare." Peterkin dolls were copyrighted by Horsman.] **(C)**

45-5 Baby Doll (left)
Fulper Pottery Co.
Flemington, New Jersey, c. 1918
13" (seated)

Bisque head on composition bent-limb baby body; open mouth with two upper teeth, glass eyes, human hair wig; swivel neck, jointed at shoulders and hips. Incised on back of head: [within vertical rectangle] "FULPER//Made in USA//9". **(D)**

Fulper Talking Doll (right)
Fulper Pottery Co.
Flemington, New Jersey, c. 1920
12"

Bisque head on composition bent-limb baby body; open mouth with
two upper teeth, brown glass eyes, replacement mohair wig; limbs
jointed at shoulders and hips; upper part of torso split for insertion of
voice box at rear, unhinged trap door covers voice box. Incised on
back of head: [within vertical rectangle] "FULPER//Made in//USA//160".
(D)

45-6 Shoulder-Head Doll
Fulper Pottery Co.
Flemington, New Jersey, c. 1920
17" (entire doll)
4½" (shoulder head)

Bisque shoulder head, cloth body
with composition forearms and
lower legs; closed mouth, glass
eyes, human hair wig; jointed at
shoulders and hips. Incised on
back of head: "[within triangle]
CMU//[within vertical rectangle]
FULPER//S-8½". **(D)**

46 | Martha J. Chase

Inspired by an Izannah Walker rag doll that she had owned as a child,
Mrs. Martha Jenks Chase of Pawtucket, Rhode Island, set out to make
a soft, unbreakable, washable doll for her own children in the closing
years of the 19th century. The result was the famous Chase Stockinet
Doll that, once a small factory was set up behind her home, became

an unexpected commercial success. The intricate and painstaking construction of a Martha Chase doll is well described by doll historian Ruth Ricker: "The head, cut in two pieces—the face and the back—was jointed at the top in a stitch similar to that used on baseballs. It was stuffed like the body for which she used tan sateen, with cotton. Head, arms, and feet were finished with flesh-colored waterproof paint. The face, which was very solid, and seemed impossible to push in, was meticulously contoured and the features painted in natural tones. The ears were well defined and appear to have been applied separately." Hands and feet were remarkably life-like, with fingers and toes individually delineated. Mrs. Chase, the wife of a physician, went on to make a wide variety of stockinet dolls, including both adult and child-size "hospital dolls," used for training nurses. Examples of her fine work follow.

46-0 Chase Stockinet Doll (color plate)
Martha J. Chase
Pawtucket, Rhode Island, c. 1900
12½"

Stockinet over mask shoulder head on pink sateen body; molded and oil-painted features, oil-painted arms and legs; jointed at shoulders, elbows, hips, and knees. Unmarked. **(D)**

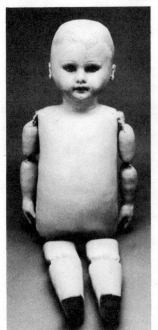

46-1 Chase Stockinet Doll
Martha J. Chase
Pawtucket, Rhode Island, c. 1910
20"

Stockinet-fabric doll with face and limbs painted in oils [see introduction to this section]; jointed at shoulders, elbows, hips, and knees. Stamped on body [under arm]: [caricature of nurse's face, with the following words on nurse's hat:] "CHASE//HOSPITAL DOLL"; [under nurse's face] "TRADE MARK //PAWTUCKET, R.I.//MADE IN U.S.A." **(D)**

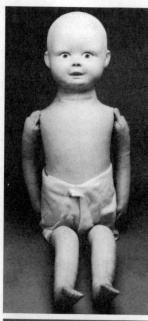

46-2 Modern Chase Stockinet Doll
M.J. Chase Co., Inc.
Pawtucket, Rhode Island, c. 1966
21"

Similar to 46-1, except that head is now made of hard rubber and body is made of a plastic fabric; jointed only at shoulders and hips. Unmarked. **(E)**

46-3 The Alice in Wonderland Dolls
Martha J. Chase
Pawtucket, Rhode Island, 1905, 1921

46-3a Tweedle-Dee and Tweedle-Dum (left and right)
12" (each)

Stockinet head [stockinet stretched over a mask and sized with glue], molded and painted features, yarn hair; cloth body and limbs, arms molded and oil-painted; jointed at shoulders and hips. Clothing sewn to body obscures any marks. Name of each character on left collars.

The Mad Hatter (center)
13" (excluding hat)

Same description as Tweedle-Dee and Tweedle-Dum, except that no name appears on collar.

46-3b The Duchess
14" (excluding hat)

Same description as Tweedle-Dee and Tweedle-Dum, except that wig is of mohair and no name appears on collar.

46-3c The Frog Footman (left)
11½"

Same description as Tweedle-Dee and Tweedle-Dum, except that wig is of mohair and no name appears on collar.

Alice (right)
15"

Same description as Tweedle-Dee and Tweedle-Dum, except that doll has molded and painted blonde hair and no name on collar. **(Entire set of six dolls, B)**

46-4 Humpty Dumpty
Martha J. Chase
Pawtucket, Rhode Island, c. 1920
15"

Stockinet head and limbs, sized with glue and oil-painted; flat painted features. Clothing sewn to body obscures any marks. **(D)**

47 | A. Schoenhut & Co.

A 1915 advertisement describes the uniqueness of the Schoenhut All Wood Perfection Art Doll with preciseness: "The Schoenhut doll is an American invention made entirely from wood. Even the head. It is perfectly jointed with steel springs. No elastic cord is used. The body, arms, and feet are made from solid wood; these parts are painted in enamel colors and can be washed. Some of the heads are modeled in the regular doll face effect to imitate the finest imported bisque heads. Character heads are artistically molded in real character style, more natural and life-like than anything attempted. It is not a doll face head, but a production of Art, executed and criticized by the most distinguished artists. The figure is jointed with our new patent steel spring hinge, having double spring tension and swivel connections—the parts are held tightly together, though flexible enough to be placed in any correct position and will stay in the position placed. The joints move smoothly. No rubber cord whatever is used in the Schoenhut doll. It will never have loose joints and will never require restringing. The feet have two holes in the soles to receive the post of our unique metal stand that goes with every doll. The one hole is straight to hold the foot resting flat, and the other hole is oblique to hold the foot in a tip-toe position. Only one stand is necessary to support the doll on one foot or the other. The shoes and stockings have two holes in the soles to correspond with those in the feet." On the following pages are a wide variety of Schoenhut dolls, from the earliest in 1911 to about the time the Philadelphia firm went bankrupt during the Depression.

47-0 Molded-Head Girl with Hair Ribbon (color plate)
A. Schoenhut & Co.
Philadelphia, Pennsylvania, c. 1912

15"

All-wood doll; closed mouth, molded and painted features and hair (parted down middle) with molded pink ribbon around head and tied in a bow at back; fully jointed (including ankles); holes for stand on soles of feet. Incised on back of body: "SCHOENHUT DOLL//PAT. JAN. 17. '11, U.S.A.//& FOREIGN COUNTRIES." **(D)**

47-1 Tootsie Wootsie (left)
A. Schoenhut & Co.
Philadelphia, Pennsylvania, 1911
15"

All-wood doll, open-closed mouth with tongue and two painted upper teeth, molded and painted features and hair; fully spring-jointed (including ankles); holes for stand in soles of feet; redressed, originally dressed as baby. Incised on back of body: "SCHOENHUT DOLL//PAT. JAN 17. '11, U.S.A.//FOREIGN COUNTRIES". **(C)**

Schnickel-Fritz (right)
A. Schoenhut & Co.
Philadelphia, Pennsylvania, 1911
15"

All-wood doll; open-closed mouth with painted teeth (two upper and two lower), molded and painted features and hair; fully spring-jointed (including ankles); holes for stand in soles of feet; redressed, originally dressed as baby. Same as previous mark. **(C)**

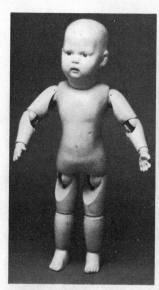

47-3

47-3 Character Boy (left)
A. Schoenhut & Co.
Philadelphia, Pennsylvania
c. 1913
16"

All-wood doll; closed mouth, molded and painted features, mohair wig; swivel head, fully spring-jointed (including ankles); holes for stand in soles of feet; original clothing. Incised on back of body: "SCHOENHUT DOLL//PAT. JAN. 17, '11, U.S.A// & FOREIGN COUNTRIES". **(C)**

Molded Schoenhut Head with Hair Bow (right)
A. Schoenhut & Co.
Philadelphia, Pennsylvania
c. 1915
14½"

All-wood doll; open-closed mouth with row of upper teeth, molded and painted features and hair; fully spring-jointed (including ankles); holes for stand in soles of feet. Green decal on back of body: "SCHOENHUT DOLL//PAT. Jan 17TH 1911//U.S.A." **(C)**

47-2 Schoenhut Boy
A. Schoenhut & Co.
Philadelphia, Pennsylvania
after 1913
13½"

All-wood doll; molded and painted features; fully spring-jointed (including ankles); holes for stand in soles of feet. Incised on head: "H.E. SCHOENHUT//©//1913". Incised on back of body: "SCHOENHUT DOLL//PAT. JAN. 17. '11, U.S.A. // & FOREIGN COUNTRIES". [Photographed unclothed to show metal spring joints.] **(C)**

47-4 Wooden Bent-Limb Baby
(left)
A. Schoenhut & Co.
Philadelphia, Pennsylvania, after 1913
14"

All-wood doll; molded and painted features, mohair wig; bent-limb baby body spring-jointed at neck, shoulders, and hips. Incised on back of head: "H.E. SCHOENHUT//©//1913". [Bent-limb babies, of course, do not have the conventional Schoenhut holes in soles.] **(D)**

47-4

Sleeping-Eye Schoenhut (right)
A. Schoenhut & Co.
Philadelphia, Pennsylvania, c. 1920
15"

All-wood doll; open-closed mouth with four upper teeth, decal sleeping eyes, mohair wig; fully spring-jointed (including ankles); holes for stand in soles of feet. Green decal on back of body: "SCHOENHUT DOLL//PAT. Jan 17TH 1911//U.S.A." **(D)**

47-5 Boy with "Imitation Glass Eyes" (left)
A. Schoenhut & Co.
Philadelphia, Pennsylvania, c. 1915
21"

All-wood doll; molded and painted features, "imitation glass eyes" (Schoenhut's term), mohair wig; swivel neck, fully spring-jointed (including ankles); holes for stand in soles of feet; redressed. Decal originally on back missing. Button: "MADE IN U.S.A. STRONG, DURABLE AND UNBREAKABLE//[within shield] SCHOENHUT//ALL WOOD//PERFECTION//ART DOLL". **(C)**

Large Schoenhut Girl with Decal Eyes (right)
A. Schoenhut & Co.
Philadelphia, Pennsylvania, c. 1915
21"

All-wood doll; open-closed mouth with four upper teeth, brown decal eyes, mohair wig; swivel neck, fully spring-jointed (including ankles);

47-5

holes for stand in bottom of soles. Green decal on back of body:
"SCHOENHUT DOLL//PAT. JAN. 17TH 1911//U.S.A." [Schoenhut's largest
dolls were 21" high.] **(C)**

47-6 Walkable Schoenhut (left)
A. Schoenhut & Co.
Philadelphia, Pennsylvania, 1919
14½"

All-wood doll; molded and painted features, mohair wig; fully spring-
jointed except legs which are single pieces of wood jointed at the hips
in a slotted fashion that enables the doll to "walk." Green decal on
back of body: "SCHOENHUT DOLL//PAT. JAN 17TH 1911//U.S.A." [No
holes in soles of feet, but soles of shoes are angled for ease in walking.
Described in contemporary advertisements as "A Doll that can be led
by the hand and will walk like a real little tot. It is one of the most amus-
ing dolls on the market." **(C)**

Composition Head Schoenhut (right)
A. Schoenhut & Co.
Philadelphia, Pennsylvania, c. 1930
14½"

Composition head on wood spring-jointed body; molded and painted features and hair; swivel neck, fully jointed (including ankles); holes
for stand in soles of feet. Incised on back of body: "SCHOENHUT DOLL//
PAT. JAN. 17. '11, U.S.A// & FOREIGN COUNTRIES." Schoenhut button as
on Glass-Eyed Boy (47-5). [Schoenhut catalogues list all-composition
dolls, but many composition heads on wooden bodies have been
found.] **(C)**

47-6

47-7 Mama Doll (left)
A. Schoenhut & Co.
Philadelphia, Pennsylvania, 1924
17"

Molded wood head and thin breast plate on cloth body with wood hands; molded and painted features, mohair wig; swivel neck (jointed with rubber elastic, not springs), jointed at shoulders and hips; voice box. Green decal on back of head: "H.E. SCHOEN-HUT//©//1913". Button on body: "MADE IN U.S.A. STRONG, DURABLE AND UNBREAKABLE//[within shield] SCHOENHUT//ALL WOOD//PERFECTION//ART DOLL". **(C)**

Character Girl (right)
A. Schoenhut & Co.
Philadelphia, Pennsylvania
c. 1920
19"

All-wood doll; molded and painted features, intaglio eyes, mohair wig; swivel neck, fully spring-jointed (including ankles); holes for stand in soles of feet; original underwear. Incised on back of body: "SCHOENHUT DOLL//PAT. JAN. 17TH 1911//U.S.A." **(C)**

47-8 Schoenhut Bye-Lo Baby
A. Schoenhut & Co.
Philadelphia, Pennsylvania
c. 1925
12"

Wooden head on cloth bent-limb baby body with wooden hands; molded and painted features and hair, "decal" sleeping eyes; flange neck, jointed at shoulders and hips; voice box. [Very few Schoenhut Bye-Los were produced.] **(B)**

48 | EFFanBEE

EFFanBEE, the wonderfully "period" trade name for the partnership of Bernard E. Fleischaker and Hugo Baum, is perhaps the quintessential example of how the American-made composition doll ("compos" to collectors) rushed in to fill the void created by the interruption of the bisque trade during World War I, eventually rose in popularity, and finally set the standard of doll production for the rest of the world. EFFanBEE's first dolls, including many versions of the successful Baby Grumpy, were described in 1920 as "long on strength but rather short in other respects," an assessment that for the time could be considered an obituary for the supremacy of the bisque doll and a prediction of the future reign of the American composition doll. Now that "compos" are remote enough in time to be highly collectible, those of EFFanBEE—with models of the '20s and '30s alone running into the thousands (400 in 1924, for example)—are much in demand. We have reached a point in time, one would think, where a **definitive** book needs to be written on the composition doll and its history.

48-O Patsy-Ann (color plate)
EFFanBEE
New York City, c. 1930
19"

All-composition doll; closed mouth, green sleeping eyes with lashes, molded hair; swivel neck, jointed at shoulders and hips; original clothing. Embossed on back of body: "EFFANBEE//'PATSY-ANN'//©//PAT. #1283558". **(D)**

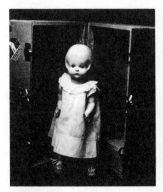

48-1 Patsy
EFFanBEE
New York City, c. 1930
11"

All-composition doll with molded and painted features and hair (blue eyes, red hair); swivel neck, jointed at shoulders and hips. Unmarked. [Photographed with original Patsy wardrobe trunk.] **(E)**

48-2 Black Patsy Jr.
EFFanBEE
New York City, c. 1930
11"

All-composition doll; molded and painted features and hair with yarn braids; swivel neck, jointed at shoulders and hips. Embossed on back of body: "EFFANBEE//PAT-SY//DOLL". On heart-shaped metal tag: "EFFANBEE//DURABLE//DOLLS". **(E)**

48-3 Patsy Babyette
EFFanBEE
New York City, c. 1930
8½"

All-composition doll with bent-limb baby body; closed mouth, sleeping eyes with lashes, lamb's wool wig; swivel neck, jointed at shoulders and hips. Embossed on back: "EFFANBEE//PATSY BABY-ETTE". **(E)**

**48-4 Colleen Moore Fairy
    Princess Doll**
EFFanBEE
New York City, c. 1930
5½"

All-composition doll; jointed at
shoulders and hips; molded and
painted features, hair, shoes, and
stockings. Embossed on back of
body: "EFFANBEE//WEE PATSY". On
button: "COLLEEN MOORE//FAIRY
PRINCESS//AN//EFF AN BEE//DOLL".
[Colleen Moore was the early film
star whose extraordinary Fairy
Castle doll house, appraised at
over a half-million dollars two
decades ago, is now housed in
the Museum of Science and Industry, Chicago. The doll was obviously made from a Wee Patsy
mold.] **(E)**

48-5 Dy-Dee Baby
EFFanBEE
New York City, 1934
16"

Composition head on rubber
bent-limb baby body, open
mouth, sleeping eyes with lashes,
caracul wig; swivel neck, jointed
at shoulders and hips. Embossed
on doll's back: "EFFAN-BEE//DY-
DEE BABY//[lists of patents for U.S.,
England, France, Germany]//
OTHER PAT. PENDING". [Doll can
"drink"; opening in body, with
plug, allows it to "wet."] **(F)**

49 | Madame Alexander

The dolls of Beatrice Alexander Behrman and the Alexander Doll
Company are so popular with modern collectors that entire books
could be written about them (and have been). The reasons for this
popularity are not hard to find. Not only have Madame Alexander
dolls been comparatively well made by American standards, but
many of them display an incisive feeling for subject matter that is
popular at a given moment. Madame Alexander has had a knack, at

least since the 1930s, for making portrait dolls of the very people and literary characters who seem to personify an age: the Dionne Quintuplets (23-0), Jane Withers (23-3), Sonja Henie (49-4), Scarlett O'Hara, and Jacqueline Kennedy (49-5) to name only a few. Moreover, Madame Alexander's dolls have remained popular because, with the passage of time, they evoke very strong feelings of nostalgia for the periods of their origin. (The W.A.V.E. and W.A.A.C. dolls of World War II (49-0), are perfect examples.) Madame Alexander's rag dolls with mask-type faces and pressed features are as eagerly collected as her later composition dolls and include characters from **Alice in Wonderland, Little Women,** and many novels by Dickens (49-1), as well as McGuffey Ana (49-3), made in the late 1930s to commemorate the 100th anniversary of the famous school reader.

49-0 W.A.A.C. and W.A.V.E. (color plate)
Madame Alexander
New York City, 1942-44
14½" (with cap)

All-composition dolls; closed mouths, sleeping eyes with lashes, mohair wigs; swivel necks, jointed at shoulders and hips. Labels on clothing missing. [Identical faces are from "Wendy Ann" mold, modeled after Madame Alexander's granddaughter and used for many dolls, including the closed-mouth Sonja Henie doll. W.A.A.C. doll is similar to "An Armed Forces Doll" made about the same time and with the same "Wendy Ann" face. Without labels they are almost indistinguishable.] **(Each, C)**

49-1 Oliver Twist
Madame Alexander
New York City, 1924-25
15½"

Cloth doll with mask face, pink muslin body; hand-painted raised features, mohair wig; jointed at shoulders and hips. Label on coat: "'Oliver Twist'//Madame Alexander//New York". **(C)**

49-2 Little Shaver
Madame Alexander
New York City, 1937
9½"

Rag doll with mask face on pink muslin body; painted features with yellow yarn hair; wire within limbs enables doll to "pose." Label on dress: "Little Shaver//Madame Alexander//New York//All rights reserved". [Based on artwork by Elsie Shaver and available in five different sizes.] **(D)**

49-4 Margaret O'Brien (left)
Madame Alexander
New York City, c. 1946
17"

49-3 McGuffey Ana
Madame Alexander
New York City, c. 1937-39
13"

All-composition doll; open mouth with four upper teeth, sleeping eyes with lashes, mohair wig with braids; swivel neck, jointed at shoulders and hips. Label on dress: "McGuffey Ana'//Madame Alexander N.Y. U.S.A.//REG. NO. 350,781''. [Face made from "Princess Elizabeth" mold as was "Snow White" and many other Alexander dolls.] **(D)**

All-composition doll; closed mouth, metal and glass sleeping eyes with lashes, reddish-brown mohair wig; swivel neck, jointed at shoulders and hips; original clothing. Embossed on back of head: "ALEXANDER". Label on dress: "GENUINE//Margaret O'Brien//Madame Alexander, N.Y., U.S.A.//ALL RIGHTS RESERVED". **(D)**

Princess Elizabeth (center)
Madame Alexander
New York, New York, 1937
20"

All-composition doll; open mouth with two upper teeth, metal and glass sleeping eyes with lashes, human hair wig; swivel neck, jointed at shoulders and hips; original clothing. Embossed on back of head: "PRINCESS ELIZABETH//ALEXANDER DOLL CO." **(D)**

Sonja Henie (right)
Madame Alexander
New York, New York, 1939
15"

All-composition doll; open mouth with two upper teeth, metal and yellow glass sleeping eyes with lashes, human hair wig, dimples; swivel neck, jointed at shoulders and hips; original clothing and skates. Embossed on back of head: "MADAME ALEXANDER//SONJA//HENIE". Label on pink dress: "GENUINE// 'Sonja Henie'//Madame Alexander, N.Y., U.S.A.//ALL RIGHTS RESERVED". **(D)**

49-5 Jacqueline [Kennedy]
Madame Alexander
New York City, 1961
19"

All-vinyl doll; open mouth, brown sleeping eyes with lashes, blue eye shadow, pierced ears, rooted synthetic hair; swivel neck, jointed at shoulders and hips. Incised on back of head: "ALEXANDER//19 © 61". Label on dress: "Madame Alexander [in script]// NEW YORK// ALL RIGHTS RESERVED". [Head modeled originally for this doll; body originally used for "Cissie" doll in 1955.] **(B)**

50 | Lenci

The pressed-felt dolls made by Enrico di Scavini of Turin during the 1920s and '30s were marketed under the name "Lenci," his pet name for his wife, Elena Konig di Scavini. Made with faces that were pressed in molds, leaving no disfiguring seams, the dolls were made in the "artistic manner" for a discriminating clientele and were dressed in high-quality clothing. Featuring hand-painted faces with eyes that always glance to the side, Lenci dolls were advertised as being popular with children from 5 to 105, a sure sign that they were intended for adult pleasure: "Every Lenci Doll is made in Italy by Italian Artists an is an individual work of art." The dolls came in a variety of designs, including peasants, milkmaids, fishermen, Pierrots, Harlequins, cowboys, Indians, orientals, blacks, policemen, soldiers, and many others including portrait dolls of Mary Pickford, Rudolph Valentino, Raquel Miller, and Marlene Dietrich. The collector should be mindful that without the original Lenci labels positive identification is not always possible; Lenci had many imitators.

50-0 Cuorinaggiore (color plate)
Enrico and Elena Konig di Scavini
Turin, Italy, 1930s
14"

Pressed felt with painted features; jointed at shoulders and hips. Tag on trousers: "Cuorinaggiore" [in script]. Tag on coat: "Lenci [in script]//Made in Italy". Label on coat: "Ars Lenci [in script]//Made in Italy Torino//New York Paris London". **(C)**

50-1 Fobello
Enrico and Elena Konig di Scavini
Turin, Italy, 1920s
19"

Pressed felt with painted features and flirting eyes (eyes move from side to side); swivel neck, jointed at shoulders and hips. Tag on skirt: "Lenci [in script]//TORINO//MADE IN ITALY". Label on skirt: "Lenci [in script]//MADE IN ITALY". Tag on skirt: "Fobello [in script]." **(D)**

50-2 Lenci Doll
**Enrico and Elena Konig di Scavini
Turin, Italy, c. 1930
14"**

Pressed felt with painted features; swivel neck, jointed at shoulders and hips; original clothing. [Labels long removed.] **(C)**

50-3 Two Lenci Dolls
**Enrico and Elena Konig di Scavini
Turin, Italy, before World War II
11" (left), 14" (right)**

Dolls are both constructed as in 50-0. Similar labels on clothing, but names of dolls are not indicated. Doll at left wears Italian peasant costume; doll at right suggests styles of late 1920s, when little girls wore enormous hair ribbons. **(Each, E)**

Selected Bibliography

Angione, Genevieve. *All-Bisque and Half-Bisque Dolls.* Camden, N.J.: Thomas Nelson & Sons, 1969.

Christopher, Catherine. *The Complete Book of Doll Making and Collecting.* New York: Greystone Press, 1949.

Cieslik, Jürgen and Marianne. *Dolls.* London: Studio Vista/Christie's, 1979.

Coleman, Elizabeth A. *Dolls, Makers and Marks.* Washington, D.C.: Dorothy S. Coleman, 1966.

Coleman, Evelyn, Elizabeth, and Dorothy. *The Age of Dolls.* Washington, D.C.: Dorothy S. Coleman, 1965.

_____. *The Collector's Encyclopedia of Dolls.* New York: Crown Publishers, 1968. (Indispensable. No collector can afford to be without it.)

Fawcett, Clara Hallard. *Dolls: A New Guide for Collectors.* Boston: Charles T. Branford Co., 1964.

Foley, Daniel. *Toys Through the Ages.* Philadelphia: Chilton Books, 1962.

Fraser, Antonia. *Dolls.* New York: G. P. Putnam's Sons, 1963.

Freeman, Ruth. *American Dolls.* Watkins Glen, N.Y.: Century House, 1952.

_____ and Larry Freeman. *Cavalcade of Toys.* New York: Century House, 1942.

Gordon, Lesley. *A Pageant of Dolls.* New York: A. A. Wyn, Inc. 1949.

_____. *Peepshow into Paradise.* New York: John de Graff, Inc., 1953.

Hillier, Mary. *Dolls and Doll Makers.* New York: G. P. Putnam's Sons, 1968.

Jacobs, Flora Gill and Estrid Faurholt. *A Book of Dolls & Doll Houses.* Rutland, Vt.: Charles E. Tuttle Co., 1967.

King, Constance Eileen. *The Collector's History of Dolls.* New York: St. Martin's Press, 1978. (An invaluable reference work.)

Noble, John. *Dolls.* New York: Walker and Company, 1967.

Revi, Albert Christian, ed. *Spinning Wheel's Complete Book of Dolls.* New York: Galahad Books, 1975.

St. George, Eleanor. *Dolls of Three Centuries.* New York: Charles Scribner's Sons, 1951.

Schorsch, Anita. *Images of Childhood: An Illustrated History.* New York: The Main Street Press, 1979.

Index of Makers

Index of Marks

I. Numerals

II. Dates

III. Letters, Initials, and Abbreviations

IV. Names and Words

V. Symbols

About the Author: Jean Bach is owner and director of the Raggedy Ann Antique Doll and Toy Museum in Flemington, New Jersey. A certified antique doll appraiser, she has contributed numerous articles to several collectors' publications. Among her recent accomplishments is the creation of a doll in honor of Queen Elizabeth II's first grandchild that she presented to Her Majesty in 1977. Jean Bach is the author of the profusely illustrated book, **Collecting German Dolls.**